I was there the morning [when] was paralyzed and he kept on preaching. It was an amazing moment, but not nearly as amazing as this book, which tells what happened after that memorable day. This true story will build your faith and help you to desire what God has in store for you, too. Read it with joy.

Eric Metaxas
New York Times best-selling author of *Amazing Grace: William Wilberforce and the Heroic Campaign to End Slavery* and *Bonhoeffer: Pastor, Martyr, Prophet, Spy— a Righteous Gentile vs. the Third Reich*

Amazing! Pastor Paul Teske might very well be one of the least likely church leaders a person would expect to understand a move of God. As a Lutheran pastor, deeply entrenched in religious tradition, Pastor Teske stepped beyond the creeds and traditions of his denomination into an open-hearted pursuit of the living God. *Healing for Today* tells how God honored Pastor Teske's pursuit by revealing himself and taking Pastor Teske and his wife, Rivers, on the greatest adventure of their lives—into the very heart and power of God Almighty.

Bruce Jacobson
Vice President, Media
Life Outreach International
Executive Producer of "Life Today" with James Robison

The God we serve is an eternal Rock of righteousness and healing, one in whom there is no shadow of turning. (See James 1:17.) I recommend to you Paul Teske's powerful book on Jesus' ministry of healing today. The insights and remarkable personal accounts he shares will inspire your heart to not only walk in healing for yourself, but to be one who spreads God's healing power to others.

Dr. Robert Stearns
Founder and Director, Eagles' Wings Ministries
Clarence, NY

Paul Teske is a walking miracle and testimony of God's love for people and the desire to see them whole. Paul is also one of the great examples I know of someone who received a miracle and then took the faith imparted to him for miracles to help others receive theirs. He has been a great blessing to me and to MorningStar Ministries and to many others around the world already. The whole world needs this message like never before: God loves us, and He is a good God who wants the best for us.

Rick Joyner
MorningStar Ministries

Rev. Paul Teske is not only helping us to understand divine healing, but he also shares from the grace to impart the same. I saw it first hand when he spoke at our church when we met in the National Stadium in Kampala, Uganda. Hundreds of people were instantly healed, including a cripple. What has touched me the most about Paul's powerful ministry of healing is the simplicity and practicality of his approach to this rather difficult subject. This is a must-read for those who want to see God's healing power work for them and through them.

Pastor Jackson Senyonga
Founder of Christian Life Ministries USA and
Christian Life Church, Uganda, East Africa

In an era where even followers of Jesus have forgotten or discount healing through faith, Paul Teske has written a powerful testimony on how the Lord has used his ministry to heal many. My wife, Kris, was diagnosed with stage-four, inoperable and metastacized cancer. I will be forever indebted to Paul for his faithfulness, counsel, and "hands on" prayers for healing, as Jesus indeed performed a miracle in her life.

This book will encourage many to reexamine their thoughts on healing and how powerfully the Great Physician continues to be available to work in lives here on Earth.

Ward Brehm
Author, public speaker, and entrepreneur
Recipient of the Presidential Citizenship Medal in 2008

The first time I met Paul, I told him "no" when asked if he and his wonderful wife, Rivers, could pray for healing for my arthritic hip. Bound by a theology that taught special gifts had "ceased" in our age, I desperately wanted—but could not find—faith to believe such a prayer would work. But my heart longed to believe, and months and a painful operation later, we met again. This time healing came not for a hip, but for my heart. The Holy Spirit flooded in, declaring himself alive, well, and powerfully active today.

A few months later, Paul was connected to a dear friend in Minnesota whose wife had been diagnosed with incurable liver cancer. Today she is cancer-free and she is another testimony to God's use of Paul in healing ministry. So, this book is true. Jesus wants to powerfully heal you and to spread healing though His Church. Read *Healing for Today* with faith-filled expectancy.

Eric Fellman
President and CEO
World Bible Translation Center

Healing for Today is a must-read for the modern mind. It's the story of how the raw power of God overcame the crippling effects of a cerebral stroke that, in the natural, was hopeless. It is an articulate, compelling, and accurate representation of the supernatural Gospel of the Lord Jesus. The reader of this book will be motivated to bring the compassion and mercy of God to anyone, anywhere. It is fresh bread from Heaven. Devour it, and let your faith rise.

Mickey Robinson
Author, international speaker, and friend

Paul Teske is a personal friend I have known for the past five years. His humility and his ministry are as authentic as the first church in the New Testament. His ministry has confirmed that Jesus is the same yesterday, today, and tomorrow.

Bill Noble
President and CEO of William Noble Rare Jewels
Dallas, Texas

Healing *for* TODAY

PAUL TESKE

BRIDGE
LOGOS
FOUNDATION

Alachua, Florida 32615

Bridge-Logos
Alachua, FL 32615 USA

Healing for Today
by Paul Teske

Edited by Christy Phillipe

Library of Congress Catalog Card Number: 2010923652
International Standard Book Number 978-0-88270-315-2

G616.316.N.m1004.35250

Dedication

I dedicate this book to:

God the Father, Son, and Holy Spirit,
to receive all the glory, honor, praise, and thanks.

Rivers,
my beloved wife and spiritual companion for life.

My wonderful children:
Tara, Paul II, and Jordan—all walking with the Lord.

My grandson, Tyler,
who is truly anointed to serve his generation.

All the saints at St. Paul Westport,
for their awesome faithfulness, love, and support
to my family and me.

Contents

PART THREE

Foreword

It was a great pleasure for me to read *Healing for Today* by my friend Paul Teske. The book gives Pastor Teske's vision for the future of the church he pastors. He writes, "St. Paul's Lutheran Church is to be a house of healing." This is his vision for every local church, as well.

This reminds me of something Kathryn Kuhlman often said when miracles happened in her meetings: "This should be happening in every church." For almost a decade Ms. Kuhlman held monthly services at the Los Angeles Shrine Auditorium, and I was privileged to have prayer with her privately prior to each service.

Now Pastor Paul Teske and his very gifted and talented wife, Rivers, are fulfilling Kathryn's prophetic words, and they are literally running with her vision. While ministering in healing, deliverance, and miracles around the world, this dedicated couple has established a working model of deliverance and healing in their own Lutheran church.

In Mark 2, we read about an incident that took place concerning a paralyzed man. The house was so full that the desperate stretcher-bearers tore off the roof to get the man to Jesus. As Paul and Rivers can attest, many people gather when Jesus, the Great Physician, is present, and those who are desperate will receive His help in so many ways.

Healing for Today shows what happens when Jesus touches people's lives, including the life of Pastor Paul Teske, who was miraculously healed of hemiplegic paralysis three weeks after he suffered a debilitating stroke. His journey of faith—from depression to deliverance—is a fabulous testimony of the power of Jesus Christ.

Yes, healing is for today, as you will discover when you read Pastor Teske's scriptural teaching and learn about many people he ministered to who were amazingly restored to health. Several of these individuals were dealing with conditions the medical profession had called irreversible and terminal.

It's wonderful to see how God reached down and called a Lutheran pastor from Westport, Connecticut, to go to the four corners of the world and proclaim that God continues to heal people today. As you read *Healing for Today*, you will be challenged, inspired, helped, and thrilled. And, if you need healing, you will find hope and faith to reach out for your own healing.

Pastor Ralph Wilkerson

Come, and let us return to the Lord;

For He has torn, but He will heal us;

He has stricken, but He will bind us up.

After two days He will revive us;

On the third day He will raise us up,

That we may live in His sight.

Let us know,

Let us pursue the knowledge of the Lord.

His going forth is established as the morning;

He will come to us like the rain,

Like the latter and former rain to the earth.

Hosea 6:1-3

Prologue

BY Kylee, a nineteen-year-old student

I'm cold. Huddled in the bottom of the shower,
the water is running off my hair into my eyes, my mouth.
But I stay,
fascinated with the fresh cuts on my legs, bright red
  tic-tac-toe marks
on my upper thighs, turning into pink water drops.
"So pretty," I say. They are mine. Just mine.
Tonight there is no hope.
There is nothing but the desire for it all to go away.

You know, this isn't the way I was meant to be. This isn't the Kylee I was born to be. I used to have motivation, willpower, and drive, even a smidge of perfectionism. Simply put, I cared. But that all seemed to disappear; just like my little brother. Here one day, gone the next. All I had left was the grief.

Softly seeping from a corner of my mind
A barbed reminder
Slicing the tender parts of my soul
Swelling and growing

1

A pressure in my chest
A bitterness on my tongue
Stealing the breath from my lungs
Until escaping from the edge of my eye
In a hot, lonely tear
Following the curve of my cheek.

And eventually, when the grief subsided, I found myself broken, an empty black hole inside of me. I felt like if you knocked on my chest you would hear an echo coming from where my heart had been. It wasn't until fourteen months after my brother's death, and four months after I had started cutting myself, that I found out that the darkness had a name: *depression*.

I was relieved to hear its name, to know that it wasn't just who I was. If it had a name it must be fixable. I must be fixable. But it didn't happen like that. Not in the first year, or the second, or even the third, where I am now. Depression has grown from a stranger living inside of me, into a scary, ugly monster version of Kylee. Like I said, I know this isn't the Kylee I was meant to be. I just keep hoping that one day the real Kylee will get to come back.

This testimony ... my story ... it isn't easy for me to tell you. It's like squeezing my heart into words and laying them on paper for everybody to judge. But I'm willing to do it for two reasons.

For *you*: the person out there who is also dealing with depression, whether it's been for a while now, or it's just begun. It really doesn't matter; pain is pain. And all I know is I would do anything to keep it from you. I don't want anyone to hurt like this, doubt like this, hate like this. But if I can't keep you from it, or take the depression from you, the least I can do is let you know that you're not the only one. I'm right here with you. When no one else understands the thoughts in your head, I want you to know that I do.

And I write this for *you*: the person without depression, who *doesn't* understand the way our brains work or how our hearts feel … because I want you to know, or at least try to know, what this is like. Maybe you'd like to help those you love with depression. Well, you can't help something you can't understand. Actually, the truth is you'll never be able to understand it, not unless you feel it. But it's just as important to know how something works, whether it makes sense to you or not. I hope I can help you with that.

BRYAN

There's always a beginning … a moment when we start changing from our regular selves into our "monster" selves, into people with depression. It isn't just there when we wake up one morning; it's not just our feeling sorry for ourselves. It's a sickness in our minds, and it always has a starting point.

Mine was Bryan, or rather, losing Bryan. I'm telling you about Bryan so that you can understand. I need you to know him like I did, so then you can know the pain that became my depression.

My family adopted Bryan from Ecuador when he was a year old and I was five. He was born with athrogryposis, scoliosis, and ciphosis. With the first, basically he couldn't bend his legs or fingers; the second two both caused a type

of curve in his back. He came to us with thick black curls and straight long eyelashes, tiny and skinny with his little brown legs sticking out in front of him. People always asked me when I was little why my brother looked different—he looked fine to me! I never saw Bryan for his physical limitations but rather for his soft heart and ridiculous sense of humor.

When Bryan was five he had to have a back surgery to fix the curvature in his spine, which would otherwise crush his lungs. After the surgery he lay in a body cast for three months with a metal halo screwed into his skull to keep him lying straight. He hunted for Easter eggs from his hospital bed that year. He finally got the body cast off, only to replace it with a body brace, which he wore for a year. When he came back from the doctor's office with it on for the first time, we were all hiding, and when we jumped out to surprise him, he almost fell over, not being used to really standing yet. But he smiled. Bryan always smiled.

I wish you could have known him; these simple, basic words don't do him justice. Bryan was a kidder, he loved making faces and laughing really loud, especially at one of his siblings. We used to sit in the living room and he'd poke my legs and tell me I had jiggly thighs. Believe me, he was the only person who could say that to me! It's only funny coming from a person who has zero body fat, I guess. Bryan didn't complain about being different. Sure, he complained about doing his math and practicing piano, but never about how his legs didn't bend all the way or how all his friends were so much taller than him. He accepted life for what it was. Bryan bowled, played catch, took swimming lessons, played piano, and could beat all of us at video games. He was as normal as they come.

The summer he was eleven, we planned a trip as a family, with some family friends, back to Ecuador so he could visit the orphanage and see the people who had taken care of him. About three days before we left, I got my driver's license. Bryan and my little sister Korin were the first people I ever drove with all by myself. Korin wanted the front seat, but I told her Bryan should get it because he was older. You could tell that made him feel pretty important. He was so short he had to scoot to the front of the seat to see out the window, but it didn't matter. We thought we were pretty awesome. We talked about how I could drive us to piano lessons now and about going to McDonald's afterward to get ice cream. It was going to be our thing.

In Ecuador, Bryan got elevation sickness, which some people get from being up so high in the mountains. He wasn't the only one to get sick and he wasn't the worst, but for him it just wouldn't go away. He did get up for one day and go see the babies; he really liked doing that. But then that night he was sick again. Mom decided it was time to take him to see a doctor. The next morning the rest of our group left to do a missions project while Mom went with Bryan. I was in a hurry to get ready, and I kept running by the couch he was lying on. One time as I rushed past, I heard him say, "I love you, Kylee." I was looking for my shoes, I was barely listening, and I just said, "Yeah, love you, too." That was the last time I heard his voice.

After we got back we could tell something was wrong. All of the adults were suddenly gone, and it was just us kids and our friends sitting in the living room waiting. I remember even thinking to myself, *What if something happened, like Bryan dying?* But then I pushed the thought away; that sort of thing wouldn't happen to us. Eventually

Melinda, who ran the orphanage with her husband, came in and sat between me and my brother on the couch. She didn't want to tell us anything yet, but we were so scared, and we kept asking her what was wrong. Finally, she put her hand on my leg and told us, with difficulty, "Bryan ... he didn't make it."

I can never tell this part of the story without crying or at least having tears come to my eyes, because those words bring back the feeling I had at that exact moment, every time. Suddenly there wasn't enough air in the room, and I felt a sensation like running into a wall. The rest of the day I always remember in senses: how heavy Bryan felt in my arms, the roughness of his pajamas, and the curve of his little chest that lay so still. The gaping silence in the driveway as I choked on my tears, clutching my knees to my chest; the taste of salt running into my mouth off of my pillow.

This is the best I can do, the best way I can explain it to you. Losing Bryan was the biggest, most consuming pain I have ever felt in my life. One minute I was Kylee and my life was a certain way, and then suddenly I was standing, looking back at what had been normal. I didn't know who I was or who my family was without my little brother. We left America a family of seven and came back a family of six.

As I mentioned before, we all have a breaking point, a moment that gives the depression an opportunity to take hold. This was mine. I don't know yours, but I'm sure whatever it was, it was excruciatingly painful and I'm sorry. Whatever happened to you, *I'm sorry*. We don't choose for these things to happen to us; we don't choose for our brains to become chemically imbalanced, for these feelings to control us. But whether we choose them or not, we still have to live with them.

It doesn't matter what exactly happened that was your breaking point. I just want you to know, this isn't your fault; *you* did not do this. And that is why you need to fight it, because this is not you.

FREE

On April 17, 2009, I walked into Caribou Coffee, hesitant and a little anxious. I was ready to believe but afraid to get my hopes up.

I sat down with Pastor Paul Teske, a man God has gifted with the power of healing and is using to remind Christians all over the world that He is a God of unimagined power. Just the other night I had been slouching in the back pew of my church, rolling my eyes and making sarcastic comments to my brother about this guy. I just didn't know if I trusted him—this whole Holy Spirit, touchy-feely stuff was kind of weird and annoying. But it was important to my dad, which was why I was there.

My parents had invited me to dinner with them and Pastor Teske after the church service, and again I complained … but I went, because they couldn't *make* me like him. It was that night though, sitting at Perkins Restaurant, when I realized that he was a human just like me and that he didn't think he was above other people. The words he spoke and the miracles that came from his words were not his, but God's. I finally knew I could trust him. Which is how I ended up agreeing to meet for a one-on-one talk.

I knew my parents were hoping I'd be healed from depression, but I went in expecting nothing. God hadn't taken the pain away for the past three years; why would today be any different?

We started out talking about Bryan, what it felt like to lose him, and how it had affected my family. Pastor Teske said I needed to give myself permission to let Bryan go and that that was not the same as forgetting him. The thought seemed to embed itself in my heart, soothing the scar I'd been carrying there for so long.

He went on to talk about giving myself permission to go after my dreams. For so long I had been too afraid of failure to even think about what I wanted to do. I'd always thought it didn't really matter, that I wasn't good enough anyway. I told him how so much of my depression had become about self-hate. He asked me to share the top three things I didn't like about myself. And after I told him he gently but firmly knocked them right down.

He reminded me that Jesus loves me as I am and has blessed me with people in my life who do as well. He has given me talents that are unique to myself, He wants to see me use them, and He truly, honestly, thinks I am beautiful. Then he talked about my needing to be so tired of the depression that I was ready to give it to God.

Throughout our talk Pastor Teske had said things that I'd already heard before, such as, "Bryan doesn't want you to hurt like this," "Jesus thinks you're beautiful as you are," and "Give your depression to God." Every time before, when someone had said these things to me, I had brushed them aside. *Whatever*, I had thought. I knew the words were supposed to bring me comfort, but they simply didn't.

But that day in Caribou, suddenly they were real. Bryan was happy; I didn't need to worry about him anymore. Bryan would want me to live my life, not to hide away in myself. As far as Jesus thinking I was beautiful, I always thought that was nice of Him, but I mean, it was Jesus, so it didn't really count. But now, knowing how stunning He thought I was, knowing He believed I was good enough … it was all I needed. I didn't need any human man to desire me to make me feel whole.

And while I had always wanted the depression to leave, at the same time the thought scared me. It had become such a huge part of me, I was afraid I wouldn't know who I was if it was gone. I thought that I would be just as pitiful and worthless without the depression as I was with it. I hated the depression, but never quite enough to let it go—until that day, the day I finally reached the point where I was so exhausted from fighting that I finally had the strength to step away. I was ready to walk away and let Jesus deal with it. I wasn't going to look back.

We finished our time together in prayer, and Pastor Teske blessed me. He gave me the words to say, telling the depression and self-hatred to leave me and go to God for judgment. I asked God to replace them with His joy and love and peace. As I said the words, I knew that when I stood up and walked away from that table, the depression was not going with me.

I walked into Caribou as a prisoner of the darkness in my mind. But when I left, I was a new girl ... I was Kylee again.

I'm back! This is the Kylee I was meant to be! Those thoughts are *gone*; those feelings are *gone*. I'm no longer afraid of tomorrow; in fact, I welcome it, because I have a purpose. I want nothing more than to obey and glorify my Lord, who rescued me from the deepest, darkest pain I had ever experienced. I haven't felt this happy, this great, in almost four years. My heart has never known this peace, this contentment. The time I was afraid to hope for is finally here.

I am free!

* * *

I continue to be expectant (not surprised) by how the Lord creates opportunity after opportunity for healing prayer. My cup of coffee with Kylee wasn't anywhere on my agenda when I traveled to Minneapolis that week. But she, dearly beloved by the Lord, became the most important person to pray with on that trip. And as a result, freedom and restoration flooded her soul and replaced the scars of depression forever. She has now been depression-free for over one year.

Kylee's first poem after her deliverance captures the essence of her newfound freedom in Jesus:

SHIMMER

My heart shimmers like pixie dust,
it trails from the crinkles of my eyes,
twirls out onto the tip of my tongue.

Do you see me?
Hear me?
Feel me?

I am here.
Just like I said I would be.

My skin is scarred,
My heart worn,
My soul weary—
But I shimmer.

Do you see me?
Hear me?
Feel me?
I am here!

My skin is now resilient,
My heart whole,
My soul replenished.

Just like I said I would be—
I. Am. Here.
Now watch me shimmer.

This is the power of the living God. This is His calling for you and for today's Church.

Pastor Paul N. E. Teske

Part One

The Stroke

The early morning air on May 7, 2004, glistened with the rising sun. As I drove to the New Canaan Society, a weekly fellowship of approximately two hundred Christian businessmen, I began to rethink my prepared text on "Christian Ethics and Morality in Business." Two hundred handouts were in my briefcase awaiting distribution to the gathering. The traffic was light this early morning, allowing my mind to envision the Apostle John on the Isle of Patmos. The man was in his nineties, and he was still waiting for the return of his beloved friend and mentor, Jesus.

I arrived at the meeting and ate the usual continental breakfast prepared weekly by a wonderful Egyptian brother. Though raised as a Coptic Christian, he had recently dedicated his life to the risen Lord and delighted in "waiting on tables" for others. As the men were called to the fellowship hall for a time of singing, I took my seat in the front. I opened my briefcase to take out the handouts, but God powerfully impressed on my heart that I was not to speak on my prepared topic. He directed me to talk about life from John's perspective as a ninety-year-old man looking back over the years from the time when he first met Jesus on the Galilean shores to his imprisonment on the Roman penal colony. I was introduced, and up I went—a man without cue cards. I opened the Book of Revelation, read the first few verses, and launched into an unprepared dissertation about John's life.

I am an animated speaker and enjoy the freedom of movement as I speak. As I shared the events of John's life, I was trying to shift my weight from my right leg to my left when I suddenly realized that my left leg could not support my weight. I continued to speak, but my mind began to race through a number of potential causes for this loss of the use of my left leg. I thought, *Is this the result of a pinched nerve? Could this be a sciatic problem?* I felt absolutely bewildered. I did not have a headache. I was experiencing no pain whatsoever. All I knew was that my leg hung like a sack of potatoes attached to my body. With no easy answer to my leg problem and because I felt no pain, I continued to talk about John for the next twenty minutes. (Only a man would do something so foolish!)

Denial is a powerful entity when it grips one's mind as it had gripped mine in that moment. As I spoke to the men, I prayed silently for whatever this was to just go away. The rising anxiety in me eventually caught up with my hopeful, yet irrational mind, and I realized this ailment was not going to improve with time. I anxiously managed to conclude my talk by gripping the podium and asked one of the brothers to come up and help me back to my seat. As I reached out to him, I collapsed. Immediately, I was surrounded by a number of men. One was a physician who loosened my tie, checked my vital signs, and began to ask me several questions. I told him that I could not move my left leg or foot.

Within minutes, the emergency medical technicians (EMTs) arrived and loaded me onto a gurney. While I was confused and nervous about my state, I remained lucid and chatted with the men around me, perhaps to hide my fear. In short order I was wheeled to a waiting ambulance and whisked off to the hospital. One of my dear brothers, Gregg Healey, asked if he could ride with me in the back of the ambulance. An EMT told him he could go with me, but he had to ride in the front seat. As we drove to the hospital, I could see another dear brother from the New Canaan Society chasing the ambulance in his red truck. I would periodically shoot him a "thumbs-up" through the window and he returned the same. I heard an EMT speaking to the hospital in preparation for my arrival; they sounded calm and not too alarmed about my condition, giving me a sense of peace.

The next thing I knew, the ambulance doors were opened, and the emergency room team hurried me into a cubicle. Within moments, a number of tubes and wires found their way into me. Gregg sat with me as the ER physician did his initial examination. He stated that my symptoms were not those of a stroke related to a blood clot, and then he asked me if I had experienced a headache or seizures. He told me that a cerebral hemorrhage usually caused a blinding headache so severe that the victim usually passes out on the spot. I told him that I did not have any pain. He then directed the staff to do a quick CAT scan to see if they could determine the root cause for the leg paralysis. As he left the curtained area, I thought about the possibility of having a brain tumor.

As I lay looking at the ceiling after my CAT scan, my lovely wife of twenty-eight years, Rivers, came into the ER cubicle. She gently embraced me with tears streaming down her face. She said that as she came through the emergency room waiting area, about fifty men were standing together in one big huddle and were praying intensely for me. A neurologist came into the cubicle and said that I had, indeed, experienced a hemorrhage in the brain. Further testing would be necessary to determine its cause and impact. Having unloaded this news, he ordered me to be moved to the critical care unit (CCU) and scheduled a MRI for the next day.

It took thirty minutes to move me and have the CCU staff settle me into my new environment with the proper connections and tubing. Then a physician stopped by to tell me that there was uncertainty as to what my final outcome might be. I remember him saying that if my brain began to hemorrhage again, medical intervention was not promising. He also told me that I should "get my house in order—just in case."

I told Rivers about my conversation with the doctor and its implications. I looked at her and mentioned that I had two requests. First, if I died, I asked her to have the congregation throw a big Easter celebration because I was home in Heaven. "If there is no resurrection, then I have been in the wrong business," I said. Second, I did not want the people to wish me back from the dead. "Once I get to Heaven, I'm staying! I am not coming back to this place," I told her. "Who would want to leave Heaven for any reason? I will be waiting for the rest of you to finally arrive. Amen." We cried and hugged each other. Then she left, due to her own exhaustion. I lay in my bed alone, thinking about what this meant for my future. "God, I am only fifty-seven years old. Am I going to spend the rest of my life in a wheelchair? Am I even going to live?" These thoughts had never before found their way into my plans for retirement.

The next morning, I awoke to a new day. I was still alive! But my left leg was still paralyzed. Other than an IV in my arm and a small oxygen tube under each nostril, I felt like my old self. All around me were people in critical shape; I appeared too normal. I asked for a newspaper, and after breakfast, they transported me to the MRI unit, where I underwent an incredible noisy procedure.

Back in the CCU, a steady stream of wonderful well-wishers came through to hear my tale and share their thoughts and prayers for me and my family. I'm not sure who ministered most to whom—the visitors or me! I spent the day speaking to my three children, who were living in various parts of the country. I encouraged my mother and other relatives that God would make a way. As uncertain as things seemed in the natural, I experienced a peace of mind that sustained me and even others as I spoke and prayed with them. I believe that I should have been a basket case, bouncing off the walls, but God gave me a supernatural peace throughout the entire ordeal. I kept thinking about Paul's words to the church at Philippi: "*And the peace of God, which surpasses all understanding, will guard your hearts and minds through Christ Jesus*" (Philippians 4:7).

On the third day, the neurologist shared with me the results of the MRI. He said that he had anticipated a malformation of blood vessels, which generally accounted for this type of cerebral hemorrhage, but the test indicated that there were no malformations or aneurisms in my brain. He said that he needed another more definitive test, one that would shoot dye into the blood vessels of the brain. The next morning, they ushered me to the angioplasty unit, where the radiologist injected me with dye. I viewed a large monitor and watched the colorful blood vessels expand through what appeared to be an outline of my skull. I asked the doctor if everything appeared to be all right, but as expected, he told me I must wait for my neurologist to give me an analysis. At least I knew I had a brain—I had just seen it!

That afternoon, my primary care physician came to the CCU to give me an update. He said that the test concluded that there were no indications as to what had caused the rupture of the blood vessel. He called it an "anatomical event." Simply put, one of my blood vessels had broken and then clotted itself. The damage to the tissue resulted from the blood flow into a portion of the brain that controlled my left side from the hip to the toes. With this diagnosis, he ordered me to the neurological ward for further observation, so after three days of MRI and angioplasty testing, and much back and forth to the CCU, they checked me into neurology to begin the next phase of dealing with my situation.

As I faced this challenge, I knew I could not get through it without prayer. God called me constantly in prayer—by myself and with others—as a way to resolve and illuminate my future. While I never felt my life threatened because I had no pain, I was unsure about a future that included a wheelchair. I asked the doctor if the paralysis would ever leave; he said, along with everyone else, "We will have to wait and see."

Even though I could not move my entire left leg, the therapist started my rehabilitation by telling me to move my big toe. He suggested that I form a mental picture of my toe moving and to try to move it in my mind. I remember trying this over and over and over again without results. But with determination to succeed and believing that anything on this side of the grave was manageable, I kept at it. Finally, after four or five days, the big toe moved! At first I thought I imagined its movement, but eventually I began to move it regularly. Nothing else moved—just the big toe, but I was elated. Within a few more days, I progressively moved my foot and then my knee. I started physical therapy to try to strengthen my leg to bear weight. They taught me to use crutches, to use a wheelchair, to maneuver various bathroom paraphernalia, and to ascend and descend stairs—all in preparation to go home. Eventually I regained about 15 percent of the use of my left leg.

On day seven, a neuropsychologist came to see me. He said that an evaluation of my mental faculties had been ordered. This angle was a new twist. He asked me if I thought such a test was necessary, to which I said, "Doc, for all I know, I could be jumping up and down on the bed right now in front of you and don't even know it! So what do you think?"

"That is the most intelligent answer I have ever heard in response to that question," he remarked.

We did the test, and I passed with no apparent cognitive damage to my brain. At least I seemed to have all my faculties.

This encouraged me, because even if I was confined to a wheelchair, I could still speak and write.

The hospital admission office constantly changed my departure date at the whim of insurance company directives. With my stay seemingly being shortened, they began rapid in-patient therapy to prepare me for my exit. Almost two weeks after my stroke, while I waited to be taken to physical therapy and pondering my future, the Lord impressed a Bible passage on my mind so intensely that I knew it related to my circumstance. I turned to Hosea 6:1-3. I did not have a clue as to what it said; I just knew it would speak to me. I had learned the difference between the *logos* (the Word), which is the written, historical document we call the Bible, and the *rhema* (word), which is God speaking through that ancient text to me in the here and now.

> *Come, and let us return to the Lord;*
> **For He has torn, but He will heal us;**
> **He has stricken, but He will bind us up.**
> **After two days He will revive us;**
> **On the third day He will raise us up,**
> **That we may live in His sight.**
> *Let us know,*
> *Let us pursue the knowledge of the Lord.*
> *His going forth is established as the morning;*
> *He will come to us like the rain,*
> *Like the latter and former rain to the earth.*
> (Hosea 6:1-3, boldface mine)

When I read, *"After two days He will revive us; on the third day He will raise us up ...,"* immediately God impressed on my heart and mind that He was going to heal me in twenty-one days. A previous prophetic word that had been spoken over me by a pastor from Ghana—Kingsley Fletcher—came to mind. According to Fletcher, God was going to do something incredible in twenty-one days; that I would have three choices and would not know at first what to do, that I would be like a kid in a candy store not knowing what to choose. That prophecy, which had been delivered four years earlier, coupled with the Hosea passage, spoke loudly and clearly to me. I knew that God was going to heal me exactly twenty-one days after my stroke.

The twenty-first day embedded itself in my soul—May 28, 2004. It was to be the date for my healing. I recorded it in my journal, shared it with my wife, and told my leaders and basically anyone who would listen. I am sure that many thought I had more "brain damage" than they had anticipated. I began to look back over my life and ponder all that I had done and not done, the good years and the wasted time. I felt like John on Patmos—looking back, yet at the same time looking forward with hopefulness in my heart. I had complete expectancy that God was going to heal me on May 28, 2004.

2

My Preparation

I was born on October 3, 1946, in Monroe, Louisiana, to Raymond and Marjorie Teske. My father served in the army in World War II and decided to settle in the South after his discharge. By 1950, he had moved the family to Waco, Texas, where he found employment at the local newspaper. He and my mother were devout Christians and became active in the local Lutheran church, with affiliations with the Missouri Synod of St. Louis, Missouri. It was there that my older brother, two younger sisters, and I attended a Lutheran parochial elementary school. In fact, we were "regular" kids, active in Scouts and Little League. My brother and I both attained the rank of Eagle Scout. All in all, we lived the *Leave It to Beaver* lifestyle of the 1950s. Most importantly, my parents laid a solid biblical foundation upon which for us to build our lives and to stand on when the storms of life would come.

After graduating from the public high school, I attended a junior college before matriculating into Baylor University. During my college years, I pushed the edge of the spiritual envelope as far as I could. I joined a fraternity and became more interested in partying than in living the Christian life. For three years, I all but turned my back on my Christian values and lived for self-gratification and amusement.

Though I knew God, I did not live for God. In hindsight, I know that the grace of God sustained me and kept me from completely falling off the planet. I believe these were, without doubt, my "prodigal years." Eventually, I left the squalor of the pigs and renewed my faith in Jesus Christ as my Lord and Savior. Thank God for the blood of the Lamb that washes away a multitude of my sins.

Upon graduating from Baylor with a BA in sociology in 1970, I faced the inevitable and invincible United States draft board. I had postponed graduation as long as I could, maximizing the number of years one could maintain an II-S student deferment. The United States, embroiled in a war in Southeast Asia, drafted thousands of young men every month for service in the armed forces. Shortly after graduation, the local draft board sent me along with sixty-five other young men to Dallas, Texas, for our physical to see if we qualified for service. Being in great health, I passed my physical with flying colors, and a Navy petty officer told me and another fifteen young men who had passed the physical, to go home and pack our bags for basic training at Fort Polk, Louisiana. He gave us four months until Uncle Sam would be calling us into his grand army. The 100-mile bus ride back to Waco seemed like an eternity. Fifty guys were celebrating, because they had "flunked" the physical. The rest of us sat gloomily dismayed and depressed. I remember thinking, *I am a survivor; I will make it through this.*

For one year, I waited nervously for my letter from the draft board to arrive, calling me into active duty. The first few months were nerve-wracking as every day I would check the mailbox. I inquired about joining the military reserves or the National Guard, but the lists were full. Eventually, I just went forward living day to day. No company would hire a person who was physically fit but 1-A draft eligible, so I worked part-time jobs to kill the time. As the war was scaling down, the nation developed a lottery system tied to birthdates for the draft. I was in the first national lottery and the number that corresponded with my birthdate was 243. At the end of that year, the national draft had only taken guys up to number 190. That was good. In January 1971, I received a letter from the draft board indicating I was no longer eligible for the draft. Now I was greatly relieved that my life could finally move forward.

Later in the year, at my mother's insistence, I attended a service at my home church. As I shook hands with the pastor, he asked me if I had ever considered the ministry as a career. I looked at him with great surprise and said, "No, sir." Internally, I thought that would be the last thing I would do, but the question embedded itself into my heart. I told my brother about the pastor's question, and he said, "Why don't you apply for the seminary? You could get out of Texas and broaden your horizons." The thought of living somewhere else appealed to me. I applied to both Lutheran seminaries and they accepted me. I picked the one in Illinois as my dad had been raised there, but beyond that sentiment, there loomed tuition and room and board at $1,800 per year. That seemed astronomical for my budget, and I decided that I could just not afford to go. God had other resources, though. Within two weeks, I received a letter from the Lutheran Texas District informing me that they would give me $800 per year to attend seminary. A few weeks later, a small church north of Waco heard about me and said they would give me a $1,000 per year to attend.

(The money had been set aside over the years to support a local candidate, but the church had never sent anyone to the seminary, and they did not want the money to go unused.) Now I had the funds—the *exact* amount of funds—so I left for the seminary in the fall of 1971, uncertain of why I was even going but certain of who was sending me.

That first fall the seminary hosted a symposium on the charismatic renewal. I attended the two-day meetings with open interest, and after the second day, ten students and one of the presenters gathered in the basement lounge of the dorm to hear more about the charismatic movement. The moderator asked if he could pray for each of us to receive the baptism of the Holy Spirit. I agreed; he laid hands on me and prayed. Nothing obvious happened. He coached us to begin to pray in tongues, but, as intensely as I tried, I could not. I left the meeting open to what had been said, but believing it was not to be for me.

The next year, I participated in a seminary abroad program in Germany to study "Reformation History and Systematic Theology." There were still no tongues, just more and more theology in my life. I returned to Illinois in 1973 for a third year of study. The next step was a non-ordained assistant pastor assignment, or internship, at the Lutheran church in Balboa, Canal Zone, in the Republic of Panama. Upon completion of my duties there, I took six weeks to drive from Panama through Central America and Mexico to Texas. This experience, coupled with my time in Europe, opened my eyes to see a world I had only previously known through television and magazines.

When I arrived back in Waco, my life changed again. Over lunch with a friend, I met a "singing waitress"—Riv-

June 6, 1976:
Rivers and
Paul on the
occasion
of Paul's
ordination.

ers Ann Hatchett—who would later become my wife. Rivers was finishing up her senior year in the music department at Baylor, seeking a degree in vocal performance. Her Christian persuasion was linked to an independent Baptist church, and it was obvious she loved the Lord. Our own love was not so obvious at first, but within two months it blossomed and we were engaged to be married. That's when things got a little hairy. I graduated from Concordia Theological Seminary in May 1976. I was then ordained June 6, 1976, in Waco, Texas; married to Rivers Hatchett

Top: *Paul in 1978.*
Bottom: *Rivers and Paul in 1988.*

on June 12, 1976, in Houston, Texas (her hometown); and was finally installed in my first church on July 10, 1976, as a church planter in North Jackson, Ohio. These were formative years for us as newlyweds trying to understand the dynamics of a marriage and a ministry. By the grace of God, we made it!

It took a few years to plant that church and to grow it to approximately 140 people. But I needed to see more of the world, and so I joined the Navy as a chaplain. For twelve years I served just about everywhere in the Navy. I consider these years my professional development years because I so enjoyed the ministry to young people. Rivers and I served two years at Philadelphia Navy Hospital. We then moved to Yokosuka, Japan, where I served as the chaplain to a guided missile cruiser with 450 men. I spent many months at sea steaming from Australia to Korea to the Persian Gulf and many places in between. By then, Rivers and I had three lovely children: two daughters and a son. Following my time on sea duty, we moved to San Francisco, where I worked directly for the chief of chaplains recruiting clergy (protestants, priests, and rabbis) for the Navy in the western ten states. From the West Coast, we moved to New London, Connecticut, where I became the protestant chaplain at the United States Coast Guard Academy. Toward the end of this tour, the Navy promoted me to commander and had issued orders for me to report to a rapid deployment unit with the Marine Corps. Rivers and I were preparing to sell our home and move to Virginia when out of nowhere came a call from a Lutheran church in Westport, Connecticut, to serve as the senior pastor. The congregation had never met me nor heard me preach. The call came sight unseen; this seemed strange.

I called the president of the congregation and made an appointment to meet with the recruitment committee. I drove the seventy miles from New London to Westport on Sunday afternoon thinking about how I would thank them but say "no thanks" to the opportunity. Approximately twenty-five folks were waiting for me when I arrived at the church. We met for a couple of hours. I listened to their hopes and dreams and told them I would pray about my decision. As I drove back to New London, I kept asking myself, *Why did you delay the inevitable? Why didn't you just say no?* When I arrived home, Rivers asked me how they had received my decision. Chagrined, I said that I had not yet turned down the offer. I proceeded to recount the meeting to her and she seemed remarkably open to the prospect of leaving the Navy and returning to civilian life.

The next week I met with the committee and told them that they had to consider some changes if they wanted to grow the church. The Westport area was only one percent Lutheran, so I told them that they needed to introduce a worship style that would appeal to a broader group of people. I also asked them if they were willing to assimilate "non-Lutherans" into leadership. I shared other progressive thoughts and ideas, and told them that I would seriously consider the call if they would be willing to make the strategic changes I suggested. In essence I was asking them to give me executive control over these decisions for one year. My terms also included a unanimous vote by the congregation. Everyone needed to be on board for this "radical" change. A week later, they called and said all my terms had been met. Confident, yet apprehensive, about the pending road less traveled, I resigned from active duty and was installed as pastor of St. Paul Lutheran Church, Westport, Connecticut, on September 10, 1989. Little did I know what God had in store for me, my wife, and the traditional Lutheran church I now served as senior pastor.

The first five years were interesting. They asked me for a mission statement. I told them that "To Know Christ and to Make Christ Known" was biblical and appropriate. Then they asked for a vision statement. After a moment of pondering, I declared, "To be a house of healing." I said that people were broken in their lives, marriages, families, etc. Little did I know the prophetic nature of that statement. We had choirs and youth groups and all the trappings of a traditional Lutheran church. More than 300 people worshiped on Sundays, and the offerings were adequate to pay the bills. My strength, power, skill base, and personality were quite sufficient to move the church forward. But I still reserved the right to my future: My ultimate goal was to wait for a church in Texas to call me to be their pastor and return to my home state to serve out my time. I also remained in the Navy reserves as a "weekend warrior" and enjoyed staying in touch with my Navy peers. All seemed grand—but God had other plans!

In the fall of 1994, the Navy chaplain corps asked me to give a presentation to the Chaplain School in Newport, Rhode Island, on ethics and morality in the Navy. The morning I arrived, I met an acquaintance, a Baptist chaplain whom I had not seen in fifteen years. As I greeted my friend, he surprised me by telling me that he "knew" I would be there that morning. I asked him who told him and he said, "The Lord!" I laughed and suggested that we meet for lunch. I met Alan at his office that afternoon for our lunch date. I again asked him who had told him I was coming, and he said that the Lord had told him in worship a couple of days earlier. His assured answer caught my attention, and I asked him to explain himself. He told me that he had been baptized in the Holy Spirit several years earlier and his life had been changed ever since. After listening to his story, he invited me to pray with him before we went to lunch. I agreed, and he began to pray. I am not sure how long we prayed, but two significant petitions of his prayer penetrated my heart.

During his prayer, he exhorted God to lift the burden of control off my shoulders. As soon as he said this, I started weeping. The weeping turned quickly into uncontrollable sobbing, and the sobbing shifted into a snot-blubbering, uncontrollable meltdown. I emotionally dumped the contents of my soul in his office. Then he prayed that God would give me the patience to wait on His timing. We prayed for a while longer and finally we went to lunch. Following a lengthy discussion over a small corner table in a local seafood dive, I bid him farewell and departed for my three-hour drive back to Westport.

While driving south on I-95, I began to pray. These prayers seemed to flow into a time of weeping. The tears and songs were intermittent without regard to content or context. All of a sudden, I heard myself speaking what seemed to be incoherent noise. I tried to stop, but I found that I had no control over my sounds. I would switch back to English for a short period, then back to the gibberish. I felt confounded and out of control. My anxiety level was rising just short of panic. It took me more than a few miles to realize that whatever this was, it was not going to subside. I continued to wrestle with my own will to manage or control the situation, but I found that I could not stop shifting back and forth between English and this noise. If this was from God, I thought, then He was going to have to convince me with a sign. I suggested he show me the number five. I looked up and saw that I was quickly approaching Exit 55 on I-95. I saw milepost 55. The speed was 55 mph! *This is too subliminal*, I thought. *I need another sign.*

"Lord, if this is really from you, let the next car that passes me have a two in the license plate." (Now in Connecticut, license plates consisted of three numbers and three letters and were rarely displayed on the front of the automobiles.) I slowed down and the next car that passed me had three "2s" in the license plate. I began to cry and praise God, because I knew that the strange sounds erupting from my mouth were the tongues of praise initiated by the Holy Spirit. I knew that the Holy Spirit had released a spiritual language in me—I was speaking in tongues! I wept, laughed, felt an incredible joy over my entire being, and continued to speak this new and delightful language.

Anxiety returned as my thoughts shifted to what awaited me in Westport. I was connected to a traditional Lutheran church with several hundred traditional Lutheran members and an ex-independent Baptist wife, none of whom believed in this stuff. My joy slowly dissipated, and my mind flooded with worry and concern. I knew that the gift I had just received was real; I also knew with the same degree of certainty that the battleground ahead of me would be difficult. I moved quite well in my own strength and power, but now I sensed that the power of God would trump anything I previously brought to the equation. I knew that the greatest test of my life rested at the end of my drive home. What I did not know in that moment, but would later come to fully realize: God would have His way!

3

New Wineskin

It is always easier to start a new church than to retrofit an old church, but with God, all things are possible. The church God called me to serve—St. Paul Lutheran Church of Westport, Connecticut—is located in lower Fairfield County, which is considered part of the New York metropolitan area. In the 1980s and 1990s, corporate executives and Wall Street bankers flooded into Westport to move their families out of the city into an upscale suburban environment. As a result, the prevailing attitude that dominates this area is self-sufficiency and intellectual arrogance. People tend to worship their "maker," and if they are self-made, then that means they exalt themselves. Some would say, "If I am self-made, then why do I need anyone else besides myself?" If God is part of their equation, He receives only minimal credit for their success. Unfortunately, much of my congregation fell into this pool of thinking.

One of the first by-products of my new encounter with the Holy Spirit was His opening up of the Scriptures for me with new insight. I began to read passages that I did not remember reading, even though I knew that I had. For example, the Bible states in James 5:14-15:

Is anyone among you sick? Let him call for the elders of the church, and let them pray over him, anointing him with oil in the name of the Lord. And the prayer of faith will save the sick, and the Lord will raise him up. And if he has committed sins, he will be forgiven.

No one taught me in the seminary to pray for the sick to be healed. My instruction included thoughtful prayers for God's will for the illness to be accepted; to pray for the doctors or for the medicines to work; to ask for strength to handle the pain; for the families to tolerate the infirmity. No professor ever taught me the instruction in James to anoint the sick with oil, lay hands on them, and pray for healing.

At the end of 1994, I approached my elders, shared the ancient text, and announced that we would walk in obedience to the mandate of James 5. One of my elders asked me if this directive was Lutheran. I told him it was biblical and we were going to do it. At the next meeting, the elder announced to the board that he had called his brother, a Lutheran pastor in the southeast, who confirmed that the anointing with oil and laying on of hands for the sick was not a Lutheran practice. But in spite of his opposition, we began a weekly healing service. The meetings started slowly and rapidly declined until it was just myself in attendance. During many meetings I would simply walk around the sanctuary and anoint the pews, walls, windows, doors, and everything else I could think of with oil. I would play praise music and pray. I believed my part was to be obedient; God's part was to bring the people.

During those early Holy Spirit years, God began to shift the church paradigm and shake us up. The first order of business for God dealt with breaking my heart for the Jews. A messianic believer who had "met" Jesus Christ in person in a vision started coming to my church. During a meeting, while he spoke about the power of the Holy Spirit in his life, God brought Romans 1:16-17 to mind: *"For I am not ashamed of the gospel of Christ, for it is the power of God to salvation for everyone who believes, for the Jew first and also for the Greek. For in it the righteousness of God is revealed from faith to faith; as it is written, 'The just shall live by faith.'"* In that moment, God's sovereignty convicted me to repent of any anti-Semitism that I every felt. God literally broke my heart for the Jews and directed me to confess my sin to my messianic friend. We embraced and wept and laughed; a new ministry door opened wide. It was a ministry that would have great impact, as 15 percent of our geographic area consisted of Jews with whom we could share the gospel of their Messiah.

We began a weekly Shabbat service to celebrate Yeshua (Jesus) as the long-awaited Messiah. Other Jewish festivals were celebrated to reveal Christ—Passover, Rosh Hashanah, Chanukah, and Yom Kippur. A weekly Bible study for messianic believers and curious Jews grew to twenty regular attendees. During a seven-year span, twenty-three unveiled Jews received Yeshua as their Messiah and were baptized into the community of faith. As we honored God by reaching out to the Jews, God honored us, the church, with blessing. But with the blessings also came attacks.

The assaults against our ministry to reach Jews for Yeshua were both internal and external. The external attacks came from local rabbis and Christian clergy in the form of meetings, editorials, and antagonistic paid ads in the local

papers. People referred to me as "Jim Jones" or "David Koresh." One full-page ad in the paper likened us to those responsible for the Holocaust. On one occasion, a member of my flock asked me how it felt to be persecuted. "If you ever drive by the church," I responded, "and see me being flogged while tied to a dogwood tree, then stop and help me. Anything short of that would be an insult to Christians around the world who are really being persecuted for the sake of the gospel. This is just the noise of the enemy; and noise is not persecution."

The internal attacks against me were more disturbing than disappointing. Members of the church would periodically come to me and not-so-politely ask me to tone down our effort to reach Jews with the gospel. When I would probe them for a reason, they would tell me that their Jewish neighbors were raising uncomfortable questions about the church's motives. Another excuse for stopping came in the guise of defending the children from our church who were receiving unflattering comments at school either from students or teachers. Still others were convinced that this new territory for evangelism was not worth venturing into for any reason. Jesus said that following Him would be difficult, and I believe He spoke prophetically over our situation. But I had concluded early on that it was better to serve God than to serve man. The complaints did not deter our efforts and as a result, some families left St. Paul.

Then God arrived one day and turned the tables over! Up until then our traditional church service consisted of liturgy, vestments, organ music, and the choir, all neatly tucked into a fifty-nine-and-a-half-minute schedule. But then, during our annual Good Friday evening service, a young man fell out of the pew into the aisle. The EMTs were called and they rushed him to the hospital. I hurried through the service and drove to the emergency room to find him fully dressed and waiting to go home. The ER staff found nothing wrong with him and discharged him. He told me that during the service, he felt overwhelmed, and the next thing he knew, he was in the ambulance. He seemed to have peace as he left the hospital.

About three months later, during a morning service, a woman collapsed and seemed unconscious. We called 911 and she was taken to the hospital. We hurried through Communion, and I once again drove to the hospital. When I arrived, she, too, was being discharged. A thorough examination by the emergency room staff could find nothing out of the ordinary. She told me that while she was on the floor in the church, she had a vision. She saw the entire front of the church full of what appeared to be a bright light. I pondered this vision and wondered what it meant.

Three months later, a woman in the choir fainted. Again, we called the EMTs and she, like the previous two "fainters," was taken to the same hospital. This time, I continued the normal liturgy. Following the service, I drove to the hospital, only to find her in good health and about to go home. All of this puzzled me greatly. In hindsight, I realize that God's presence had interrupted the flow of the service. He purposefully was breaking the rubric of the liturgy. And since I had never before seen anyone fall under the power of God, I had no point of reference to explain what was happening in my church. All I knew was that God was somehow responsible and it produced in me an obsessive need to move forward. Like Richard Dreyfuss declared in *Close Encounters of the Third Kind*, there was no turning back. It would be a few years before I would fully understand what God was doing at St. Paul. During that time, God honored our obedience.

The first healing launched my church to yet another level of spirituality. It started when I received a frantic call from a young mother who had just given birth to her second child. I rushed to the hospital to find the father hovering over his wife's bed while she held their newborn son. What should have been a happy event had turned tragic when they were told that their newborn was a dwarf with a certain condition that would prohibit his internal organs from developing. I consulted with the medical staff, and they said the baby would only live five to six months. Returning to the parents, I asked if I could hold the baby as I prayed. We definitely needed to pray. I closed my eyes and heard myself say, "Lord, I know that you are going to completely heal this baby. He will grow up and live a normal life." As I said this, I thought to myself, *You* jerk! *Why are you saying this? You don't believe this!* I was afraid to open my eyes, because I thought the parents were going to be angry with me for saying something so bizarre. Slowly I opened them, only to see the parents staring at their son, not responding to my prayer in any way. As I left the room, I remember wondering if I really had said what I thought I said or if I had just imagined that I said that prayer.

Two days later, the mother called me. She blurted out that the tests had been wrong! According to the doctors, the baby did not have the terminal condition. Her son was still a dwarf, but he was not going to die. I thanked the Lord that the tests were wrong and that the child was going to live.

But the healing didn't stop there. One month later, the phone rang. I recognized the mother's voice, but this time she was sobbing so hard, I could not understand a word she was saying. I immediately drove to her home thinking that the original test was right and that the baby was going to die. I knocked on the front door, but there was no answer. I went around to the back of the house and saw her standing in the middle of the yard with the baby in her arms. When she spotted me, she ran over sobbing and still not telling me any details. I held her in my arms, asking the Lord why He would do this to this family. Then she said something that forever changed my faith. She said, "Pastor, the baby is not a dwarf!" What we experienced in that child was not merely a false test result, but a powerful and loving act of God.

Unsolicited, God took an old wineskin and began to remake it into something new. The process was confusing and His motives were often unknown, but we stepped forward anyway. In those days I taught a men's Bible study on Saturday mornings. As this group was of a questioning mind, I introduced them to a book that someone had given me, *They Speak in Other Tongues* by John Sherrill. After several weeks, I suggested that we visit a Pentecostal-style church. The only service I could find in the area that did not conflict with our Sunday morning service was at a small Vineyard Church near Westport that had a monthly Friday night service. Eight men agreed to attend the service, so we loaded up two cars and headed for the "Hearts of Fire" service. We entered the small Vineyard Church and saw about fifty chairs facing a small stage, but the audio speakers were the size of two large garage doors! The middle-aged minister stood up and welcomed everyone, and then he sat down. The band cranked up, and we spent the next hour drenched in blasting praise music. I thought it would be a miracle if my guys just lasted through the music!

After the musicians retired, the minister again stood up and directed the group to push the chairs against the wall, because we needed the room to accommodate what God was about to do. A number of people quickly moved to the front, and as he touched them, they fell back into the arms of those standing behind them. My band of brothers stood back, observing a lot but saying very little. The minister walked up to one of my men and asked him why he was shaking, not on the outside, but on the inside. Then he said that God just wanted to touch him with His love, and he asked if this would be all right. My friend agreed. A simple touch to his chest and down my congregant went like a ton of bricks. Four of the eight St. Paulers were slain in the Spirit that night. (And no ambulances were called in response!)

During the next six months, I took approximately seventy people to that Friday night service. I knew that the power of God was moving in that venue and that my people would be touched. About two-thirds of our congregation experienced the power of God in their lives in a profound way. But unfortunately, several members left the church because it was too much for them handle. One who wanted to leave, but could not because of her situation, was my wife, Rivers.

4

Rivers of Living Water

Someone once said, "Behind every great man is a great woman." I am no exception. Aside from God, my best supporter on the planet is my wife, Rivers. She followed me from Texas to the East Coast to Japan to the West Coast and back to the East Coast again. Multiple moves and raising three children while I was deployed to sea (sometimes for months at a time) qualified her for the spouse's Medal of Honor. But even though she loyally followed me everywhere geographically, the spiritual transition into the baptism of the Holy Spirit did not come easy for her. In fact, she would agree that she did not come to it short of kicking and screaming.

When I returned home from my experience of being baptized by the Spirit in 1994, she was confused and concerned. The "hellfire and brimstone" independent Baptist church background quickly shot to the surface. She declared, "We don't believe in that stuff! What will God think?" She would later say that even though she did not understand what was going on with me, she trusted me. She knew that if I truly believed this to be from God, then she would trust me and blindly follow me down this path. She tried to remain open to what God wanted for her—and for us.

Several spiritual encounters happened to prepare her to be filled with the Spirit; however, two special events were pivotal. While cochairing the first Connecticut Prayer Breakfast in 2000, a friend told her about a tribal king from an African country who was to speak at the state capitol gathering and suggested that she go to evaluate the event. She agreed, and we drove to Hartford on Thursday of Memorial Day weekend. The African speaker, Kingsley Fletcher, seemed to be a very godly man and gave a powerful testimony about his faith. We learned that he would speak at a large church in Hartford that evening, so we decided to stay to hear him speak again and then return to Westport after the service.

The next morning, a woman from the organizing committee called and invited us to join her and Kingsley for lunch in Hartford. We were intrigued and accepted the invitation, so back up to Hartford we drove. We met them at a restaurant and listened as he shared portions of his life story. Time flew. We were so engaged in his message that we spent another three hours after lunch just walking and talking. It was an unexpected blessing. Returning to his hotel, Kingsley invited us to attend yet another service that evening at a large Hispanic church in Hartford. We were happy to accept his invitation.

Upon arriving at the church, we were ushered to the front row, where we observed the pastors and wives going to the altar to labor in prayer before the service. The room became packed with about 700 people. Worship and prayer preceded Kingsley, who then delivered a mighty word from God. We were just into the service when a large man came stumbling down the aisle, blatantly disrupting the service.

A host of ushers surrounded him and were dwarfed by the man's superimposing frame. Kingsley, seeing the disruption for what it was, rebuked the demons and the man went floundering to the floor right in front of us. I, along with several others, began to pray for him. I knelt down and placed my hand on his chest. With froth coming out of his mouth, he looked at me and said, "Paul is going to die." I could not believe my ears. He then was lifted up and ushered out.

Kingsley resumed speaking, but then he stopped and looked at me. He told me to stand up. I did, and as I stood in front of him, he began to prophesy. He said that God was going to do something in twenty-one days and at the end I would have three doors open to me; I would feel like a kid in a candy store, not knowing which door to go through. Without any warning, I collapsed and fell backward, slain in the Spirit for the first time. He resumed his sermon as I lay there and eventually, when I could, I rejoined Rivers on the front row.

At one point, Kingsley stepped down from the platform to bless all the pastors and their wives in the row opposite us. He then returned to the platform and continued to speak. Rivers whispered to me that she was disappointed because he had not come to our side to bless us. As he was nearing the end of his talk, he took off his jacket and placed it over his arm. Now finished, Kingsley stood there in silence. We all waited in the silence, too. And then, as if the entire night was about this very moment, he said that there was one more person God wanted to touch. I nudged Rivers and said, "I believe he is speaking about you." After a long pause, Rivers got up and walked to the front of the stage. She stood there, eyes closed, tears streaming down her face. Nothing happened. The room was completely silent. After a few moments, she thought that maybe he was speaking about someone else and she was just about to leave when he took his jacket and gently draped it over her head. She fell down and began to sob uncontrollably. As soon as Rivers hit the floor, pandemonium broke out. People started rushing forward and God touched over 500 people that night.

She lay there for two hours. Rivers later said that she had seen a man dancing with a flag when the worship started and in her heart she had questioned his motives. She thought he was ridiculous. Later, while she was lying on the floor, she opened her eyes and the same man was on the floor next to her. She said the man looked "beautiful," and she repented for being so unfairly judgmental.

There is no doubt that God touched both of us that night. I received the "Twenty-one Day" prophecy, and Rivers received a breakthrough in the Holy Spirit to move to a deeper place.

The next major episode to shape Rivers's spiritual heart came on our trip to Toronto in January 2001. It started when a woman from our church gave me a check for $3,000 and told me to take Rivers and other church leaders to the Toronto Blessing. I agreed, and we planned a trip to attend the Father's Heart conference in January. By this time, Rivers was desperate for God to reveal himself to her. The power of God had touched her and His peace had broken off much confusion, but she still needed something more, more intimacy from God. She wanted proof that He was real.

All her life, she had felt abandoned and rejected. She came from a broken home and longed for her earthly father's love and affirmation. For some time she had been crying out for a sign from God. She had followed me down the charismatic path as the Holy Spirit invaded our lives. She prayed fervently that a sign from God would confirm the validity of what I was saying about the Holy Spirit. "Lord, just use my name: Rivers. No one else will know," she said. "It will be between you and me." She hoped that someone on Christian television would say, "And there is a woman named Rivers out there who ..." She did not care how, but she believed that if her unique name was used, she would know it was from God.

We loaded the church van and left for Toronto a day early because of a pending blizzard that was forecast to move across the northeast. But even with the extra twenty-four hours, as we departed Westport in the afternoon, the snow began to fall. By the time we reached upstate New York, the snow blurred the freeway. About midnight, drained by slow progress and struggles with weather, we decided to pull off the highway for a meal. We made a random right turn and headed down a dark, snow-covered road in search of an open restaurant. After driving several miles and not finding anything, we decided to turn around and head the other direction. As we made a U-turn, Rivers looked out the window and saw a little shack that was closed for the night. The sign above the door said "Angel's Restaurant—Fried Chicken." Fried chicken had always been her favorite food. Then she saw something that stunned her. A large marquee with multiple blinking lights illuminated the falling snow. There were two words on that sign: RIVERS WANTED. She could not believe her eyes. She had asked for a sign with her name. She burst into tears. No one knew why she was crying, but she did. God had given her heart's desire: a sign using her name. God, her heavenly Father, indeed wanted her! Rivers said later that she had never seen her name, *Rivers*, in the word *drivers*. (At the snow-covered fried chicken restaurant, the *D* had fallen off the sign so it said "Rivers Wanted" instead of "Drivers Wanted.") She chose to keep the moment to herself and pondered it in her heart like Mary.

After twenty-four grueling hours on the road, we arrived at the Toronto Airport Fellowship Church to attend the Father's Heart conference. The first day, we sat in our assigned seats and the worship began. Rivers had not shared the encounter she had with God via the sign, and she still was not completely open to what God was doing with my congregation and me. At the opening of the Father's Heart conference, Rivers noticed strange animal-like bobbing and weaving behavior from several people, who seemingly were trying to worship. "This is too much to take. I am out of here," she told me. I strongly encouraged her to stay and ignore the distractions. Fortunately, she stayed.

One of the presentations was on the Father's love, which was right up Rivers's alley. At the end, the speaker invited pastors and wives to come forward for a blessing. Routinely, 200 couples went up and stood in front of a large stage. I felt led by the Spirit to walk up on the platform to ask the speaker if he would please come down and pray for my wife, Rivers, to receive an impartation of the Father's love. He agreed and came down to where she was waiting. A perfectly timed vehicle to heal her brokenness, he asked her about her relationship to her father. Issues of rejection, abandonment, unforgiveness, sadness, shame, guilt, and other variables came percolating to the surface. One by one, they were released until they were gone. Then he asked her if she could trust her heavenly Father. After years of struggling and even more that night, breakthrough came for her. Winter imparted the Father's love to her and the outpouring of the love from His throne poured into Rivers, sealing the Holy Spirit in, with, and upon her. She exploded with joy! She could not be contained for the rest of the conference. The man then prayed for me and gave me an impartation to give the "Father's Love" to others. This prayer has been a powerful part of my ministry for the past nine years.

Rivers went on to be filled with the Holy Spirit, speaking (and even singing) in tongues. God has given her a seer gifting, which flows regularly in revelatory prophecies. Once God yoked us together, He initiated the next level of our ministry, both at St. Paul's and around the world.

5

No Turning Back

*If you will not hear, and if you will not take it
to heart, to give glory to My name," says the* LORD
*of hosts, "I will send a curse upon you, and I will
curse your blessings. Yes, I have cursed them already,
because you do not take it to heart.* (Malachi 2:2)

The next four years were battleground years. Sometimes
I felt like I had experienced more *coup de grâce* than
some African nations. Every demonic spirit available came
against the healing ministry in my church. But God had a
plan that would not be thwarted by demon or human. One
significant turning point followed the Toronto experience.
I invited the pastor who had blessed us with the "Father's
Love" to spend a weekend with my elder board in February
2002. I wanted him to impart the Father's blessing to my
leaders. He arrived on a cold Friday and spent that evening
and Saturday morning with the nine of us. On Saturday
afternoon, he shared an unbelievable story. It started by
him opening his mouth and showing us his teeth; among
the regular teeth were two gold and one platinum. He said
that he had gone up for gifting prayer in his church and
following the prayer, three of his teeth had changed into the
precious metals. (He went to the dentist, who verified that

he had not put them in his mouth and that they did appear to be gold and platinum.) As he was sharing his story with us, I was thinking about alchemy, the Dark Ages art of turning metal into precious metal. How was this possible? Why would God do such a thing? The pastor then asked if we would like to receive a similar gift from God. Here was a moment to test or bolster our faith.

We all looked at one another with amazement. I was the first to speak. "Can I be completely candid with you? You are either telling us a true story or you are telling us a lie. There is no in-between in this. Now, you have been with us for two days, and I do not believe you would make this up. So, I believe you are telling us the truth." I looked at the others and asked them if they wanted to pray that God would give us a gold tooth. We unanimously agreed that if God desired to do that, then we would receive it.

The pastor then asked if anyone had any dental issues. One man said that his spouse had some issues, but the rest of us had pretty fit mouths. The guest speaker then told us to look in each other's mouths to affirm normal, calcium teeth, so we would know for certain if someone received a gold tooth after prayer. I looked in a man's mouth; he had no gold teeth. He looked in my mouth; I had none. A man looked in the mouth of a wonderful elder in his late sixties who had been in the church for more than thirty years and had weathered the storms of change. Though he felt thoroughly stretched by all the changes, he loved the Lord and had stayed the course with me. The examiner found two gold fillings in the older brother's mouth. I also looked in his mouth and saw two gold filings in two top teeth. I then scanned the rest of his teeth and saw no other gold.

(I thought to myself, *He has pretty good teeth for a man his age.*)

The guest speaker encouraged us by saying that if God gave someone a gold tooth, the joy would be inexplicable, and we would all share in the joy regardless of who received a gold tooth. He then gave a short prayer. (I cannot remember what he prayed. At the time, I was so worried about whether we were doing the right thing or not, I was saying my own prayer for the potential need for God to have mercy on me and forgive us if we were sinning.) When he finished praying, he told us to look in each other's mouths to see if God had given someone a gold tooth. My friend and I examined each other and saw no gold. Then the man who had examined the older elder's mouth spoke up and declared that he saw a gold tooth. The man agreed, "I know; I have two gold fillings." The other man clarified, "No, you have a *new* gold tooth."

"Let me look," I said. When I looked in his mouth, I saw a bright, shiny gold tooth in the lower left side of his mouth that went from gum line to gum line. "You really do have a gold tooth!" When he looked in the mirror, his knees buckled. This gold tooth was an incredible, amazingly unexpected miracle, and all the church leaders witnessed it. After a time of elation and wonderment, we left to go to our homes to collect our spouses for dinner and planned to return to my house later in the evening.

I went home and told Rivers. She could not wait to see the tooth. Later that evening, the elderly gentleman and his gold tooth arrived at my house early and alone. I asked him where his wife was, and he said she was not coming. He related to me how he had returned home and told her about his gold tooth. Instead of rejoicing, she bristled with anger and challenged the wisdom of such a thing. And finally, she refused to come. Interestingly, he said that while he was talking with her, he noticed something sparkling in her mouth. (His wife had been mentioned earlier in our prayer requests as the person needing dental work.) He said, "I believe you have something in your mouth." When she opened her mouth, he saw four new gold teeth! I asked him what she said when he pointed it out to her, and he said that he was afraid to discuss it with her.

That night, we gathered to meet the guest and hear the story about the gold tooth. Everyone lined up and looked into his mouth and pondered the meaning of this extraordinary miracle. The miracle excited some and turned others completely off. Either way, it was what it was and could not be reversed or denied.

A couple of weeks later, the man who had received the gold tooth came to me and felt that he should give his testimony to the whole church. I suggested the next week, Palm Sunday, as everyone would be there and all needed to hear his testimony. Palm Sunday came, and my elder told his story. People lined up to see his tooth. Again, some were turned off and eventually checked out of the church. (I believe God prunes His trees, and this was a divine pruning.)

The question was asked, "Why would God do something like this when people are dying of cancer?" I am sure people outside the wedding at Cana were dying of illnesses, but Jesus still changed water into fine wine. God has a purpose for everything He does. The Bible speaks of signs, wonders, and miracles. A "wonder" is something that leaves an indelible imprint on your mind. The gold tooth miracle certainly did that for St. Paul. I believe God gave us a wonder. Let us wonder about it! Since then, whenever the church has faced any issue that seemed difficult in the natural realm, people will say, "Remember the gold tooth." It became a real faith builder.

Most importantly, I believe God was giving us a test. He says in the Word that if you can be trusted with a little, then you can be trusted with much. If we were not able to handle this little gold tooth miracle, why would God waste His time doing the greater signs, wonders, and miracles that were to come to St. Paul? This "wonder" required us to remember three things about God:

He is good.

He knows what He is doing.

We can trust Him.

As I opened up more to God, He started putting people of influence into my life. One morning, I rose early to have a cup of coffee and watch the morning news. I surfed the television stations and came upon a man talking about Jesus. I listened to him speak about healing and deliverance, and at the end of his program, he said, "If you need healing prayer, put your hands on the TV." I immediately thought of the healing evangelists of the 1950s who were broadcasted in black and white. They would shout and tell you to put your hands on the television and be healed. As a kid, I remember my pastor saying these men were of the devil and not of God. But this day I thought, *Okay. I will do this. Let's see.* I had just been tested for sleep apnea—a breathing disorder— and the prognosis was that I had a mild case, not warranting further treatment. I thought, *If this man prays for this specific ailment, then I will know he is a man of God.* I placed my hands on the TV, and he prayed for several things, but not sleep apnea. *Why am I wasting my time?* I thought.

As I was backing up to sit on the sofa, the man stopped, looked out of the TV right at me, and said, "There is a man watching right now with a respiratory problem, and if he will not mock healing, God will heal him." As soon as he said that, I started to weep. I knew this message was from God to me. When you have sleep apnea, you do not experience REM sleep. Instead, you can only dream during ninety-minute cycles. Prior to that broadcast, I had not dreamed, but after that prayer, I started dreaming frequently. I had been healed. The man on television broadcast was Benny Hinn. I immediately went to a Christian bookstore and found a book titled *Good Morning, Holy Spirit*, written by him. This marked the beginning of my journey with Pastor Benny Hinn.

In August 2000, Rivers and I attended our first Benny Hinn Miracle Crusade in Worcester, Massachusetts. It was a Friday evening and we were curious; we wanted to see firsthand what was taking place there. Rivers and I were desperate for God's presence without fully realizing our hunger and need. We drove four hours to stand in line four hours to attend a four-hour service, only then to drive four hours home. I still cannot believe we did that.

That experience sparked more curiosity, and Rivers and I attended another Benny Hinn event—the Partners Conference in Charlotte, North Carolina, in October 2000. At one point during the seminar, Benny randomly walked over to us and said, "God is going to put fire on your lives."

He then touched us and we fell out in the Spirit. Later at the conference, I stood in the lobby watching Benny Hinn sign books for two women. In that instant, God clearly spoke to me about Benny Hinn and a future relationship we would have.

Fast-forwarding to August 2003, at that time Rivers and I attended a dynamic, miraculous Benny Hinn Crusade at Madison Square Garden. This time we brought more than ourselves; we brought a need. A young person who had been attending my congregation agreed to attend the crusade with us. This individual had been struggling with cancer for several years, and the cancer had metastasized to his brain, lungs, liver, and bones. The infirmity had made it difficult for him to stand or sit for any length of time. We literally brought the patient into the arena on a pallet, just like the four men brought their paralytic friend before Jesus in Mark 2. However, during the crusade, this person was totally healed, and the cancer markers eventually returned to normal. This healing testimony strengthened the church, and many people have been blessed through this witness.

6

Final Preparation

From that moment, Rivers and I began to intersect with a number of influential and godly people. Most importantly was our introduction to Harald Bredesen in 2000. An acquaintance familiar with the experiences we were having told me of a Lutheran minister who was speaking at a neighboring charismatic church. My curiosity piqued, I attended the gathering, only to meet another Spirit-filled Lutheran clergyman. I desired to share what was happening to me, but I could not find many Lutheran brethren who could relate. There just were not many around at that time. I arrived at the meeting and sat near the front, more than ready to soak it all in. After the praise time, the local pastor stood up to introduce Pastor Harald, but to his dismay, his guest speaker had disappeared. After a brief search, they brought him forward and gave him a rather lengthy introduction, part of which included claiming he was the father of the 1960s charismatic movement and that he had coined the term *charismatic*.

I was surprised by the power that erupted from this small man who stood about five feet tall. Before Harald spoke, the sponsoring minister asked people to come forward in faith with an offering and literally lay it at Harald's feet. I joined the long line of those going forward to honor him,

*Paul and his mentor,
Harald Bredesen.*

and when I reached Harald, I introduced myself as a fellow Lutheran pastor. He exclaimed, "So am I!" Exactly the reception I had desired. Following the service, we made an appointment to have lunch the following Tuesday. Little did I realize that this meeting would be the beginning of a powerful friendship.

Over Tuesday's lunch, Harald shared his life story with Rivers and me. What a story! He had been raised in Iowa in a Norwegian Lutheran home. His grandfathers, uncles, and father were all Norwegian Lutheran pastors. He attended a Lutheran seminary, but after graduation in 1944, he chose not to be ordained as a Lutheran pastor. Instead, he moved to New York to pursue a para-church ministry, and in 1946, he was baptized in the Holy Spirit at a Pentecostal camp meeting. His life was changed forever.

Harald, like me, was called to a small congregation at a Dutch Reformed church in the New York area. But the church did not stay small for long. At the Dutch Reformed church, he hired a newly ordained Pat Robertson to serve as his assistant minister. His charismatic leadership fostered relationships with Norman Vincent Peale, David Wilkerson, Oral Roberts, Benny Hinn, John Sherrill, Pat Boone, Anwar Sadat, and many others. It was during these early years that Walter Cronkite featured Harald's church on national television and brought the charismatic movement into twenty million homes in one evening. Eventually Harald left the New York area and settled in southern California, where he based his ministry and from which he impacted the world.

After lunch, Harald asked Rivers why her husband had not asked him to be his mentor. My wife answered, "My husband would not be that presumptuous." A divine idea was born. Just a few weeks later, Harald spoke in my church, and at the end of his sermon, he surprised the congregation (and me) by asking if he could be our pastor-at-large. I asked the folks what they thought, and they unanimously said, "Yes!" From that moment forth, Harald would introduce me as his "boss" and himself as my "mentor." I believe what he sowed into me and my ministry was divinely supernatural. We had an Elijah/Elisha relationship spanning more than seven years and graced with innumerable blessings. Harald was an original in the Spirit. (He passed away in December 2006.)

In early August 2003, Rivers helped produce Harald's eighty-fifth birthday party in Los Angeles. It was quite an event and proved a great forum for meeting a number of charismatic leaders for the first time. One such person was a young man of Malaysian-Chinese descent who, after dinner one night, asked me if we could talk privately. He said that he had a prophetic word for me. Our meeting started with him first asking permission to pray for healing for me. I encouraged the prayer, and he told me that God was healing my right knee. This statement amazed me. Many years earlier, I had snapped my ACL (anterior cruciate ligament) while playing football. Over the years I had learned to cope with the injury and even wore a knee brace for sports. However, in recent years, the cartilage in the knee had worn down and was giving me much more discomfort, especially at night. My orthopedic surgeon told me that eventually I would need knee a replacement to rectify the problem, but I was just dealing with it when the young man prayed.

Rivers and Paul with Pastor Benny Hinn at the eighty-fifth birthday celebration of Harald Bredesen.

He then told me that God had revealed to him that I had a cardiovascular issue, as well as a problem with my kidneys. Chin said God would cover these and take care of them. I thought he might be referring to a minor case of hypertension (high blood pressure) and to kidney stones (of which I had a history). After the healing portion of his prayer, he released a rapid-fire prophetic word for me. Though at the time, I reflected deeply on the words as they poured forth, today I have very little recall as to the content of the message. However, the outcome of his healing prayer will never be forgotten.

After that evening, my knee discomfort ceased. To this day I have not had a problem with my right knee. God instantly restored my knee, so that I have no pain—and so that I would begin to understand Him as our Lord who heals. Concerning the other two areas of prayer, eight months later, I experienced a major cardiovascular event—a cerebral hemorrhage, the stroke I have already described to you. Two months after my stroke, a kidney stone managed to lodge itself in my urethra (the tube between the kidney and the bladder), which a urologist surgically retrieved three days later. In hindsight, the young prophet had declared and decreed my physiological destiny. Again, to the glory of God!

That prophetic experience was in early August 2003. After that I experienced the Benny Hinn Crusade, in which my congregant's cancer was healed. And on March 26, 2004, I was sitting with two hundred businessmen at the New Canaan Society, where they met weekly for song, fellowship, and a Christian message. A man who was attending that morning came up to me after the meeting and told me that he had been drawn to me—and it was an important and divine meeting for me. He shared a word from God that had struck him when he first saw me in the crowd. He said that this was the time for me to break out and move forward. "Do not hold back; for whatever reason, you have been holding back. Do not hold back," he said. This confirmed *verbatim* the word to "go out" that Rivers and I had received in the months prior via prophets like John Paul Jackson and others.

So Rivers and I began to earnestly pray over this prophecy and seek the Holy Spirit's guidance. I kept thinking about the "twenty-one" days that Kingsley Fletcher had spoken to me four years earlier. As I was praying, the strangest thought came to mind. This date, March 26, 2004, was approximately four years after Fletcher had given me that prophetic word in Hartford, Connecticut. Kingsley had given me the "Twenty-one Day" prophecy on Friday, May 26, 2000. I calculated the number of days between these two encounters, and what I concluded seemed so strange that it even astonished me. I began working with the dates; four years was forty-eight months or 4 times 365 plus one day for Leap Year. This equation equaled 1,461 days less 61 days for April and May. The exact number of days between these two prophetic words was 1,400 days. I shared this finding with Rivers as it seemed like such an odd number, but not a random one.

While I was pondering the 1,400 days between Kingsley's "Twenty-one Day" prophecy and the other man's prophetic words, Rivers cried, "Come look at this!" Perplexed, I scurried over to the table where she was sitting. She said, "If you divide 21 into the 1,400, the answer is 666.666 *ad infinitum.*" Initially, we thought this must be the end of Satan's attack on our lives as the attacks of the enemy had progressively grown stronger since the first prophecy in 2000. We felt relieved.

But it really was a warning of what was yet to come. A signal of clear and present danger came in the spring of 2004 from a new voice of God. A dear friend and man of God, Denny Fitzpatrick, the general manager of the Beverly Hilton Hotel, introduced me via telephone to Jane Manley. We became instant friends, and she and I spoke often about what the Lord was doing in our lives. Occasionally, Jane would be led to give me a prophetic word over the phone (which I would tape, with her permission, for future prayer and reflection). On May 4, 2004, we were speaking and she began to prophesy. During the middle of her prophetic stream of words, she cried out for God to "protect my head and to dispatch angels to safeguard me." Three days later, on May 7, 2004, I experienced my stroke.

7

Healed to Be a Healer

Thirteen days after the stroke, I was released with a brace and walker to an outpatient therapy program. The medical world's "prescription" was therapy, and months of it. But God had another timetable for my recovery. Deep in my spirit, I knew God was going to heal me, and a Scripture passage God had given me several days earlier secured my hope. It was Hosea 6:2: *"In two days He will revive us; on the third day He will raise us up."* I began to dwell on this word.

On Friday, May 21, Reinhard Bonnke was scheduled to speak at the New Canaan Society and I was determined to go. I had already made arrangements with the hospital to give me a day pass to attend, but since I was now released, I asked Rivers to drive me to the 7:30 A.M. meeting. I was getting ready in the morning and asked her for my watch, which I had not used since it had been taken from me at the hospital. She said it was locked in my briefcase along with my cuff links, and she handed me the case as we were leaving our driveway. I took out the watch and noticed that the hands of the clock were not moving. It read 7:58— May 7. I thought that it was strange for a self-winding watch to stop at the exact time I started to speak on the day I had my stroke. I turned the hands forward, thinking that it had

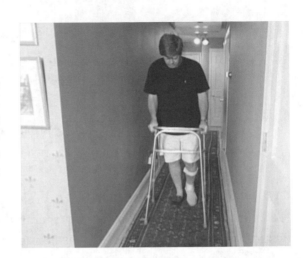

Thirteen days after the stroke, Paul was released with a brace and a walker.

stopped later in the day, at 7:58 P.M. However, when the hands passed twelve o'clock, the date did not turn over to P.M. time. "My watch stopped at approximately the moment I had my stroke," I told Rivers. Perhaps she had moved the briefcase around and it broke, but that would not make any difference for I had worn the watch at least thirty minutes after I had the stroke. I pondered this as we drove to hear Bonnke. What was the significance of my watch stopping and then allowing me to witness this phenomenon? Was God revealing that He controls the hours of the day? I shook my watch and it started running again.

I sat in the front row at the New Canaan Society meeting. Fourteen days had passed since I had stood before this very audience. The society's moderator invited me forward to say a few words, and I moved slowly toward the podium using a traditional, four-legged walker and a brace on my left foot to keep my toe from drooping. After receiving a standing ovation, I shared that it was by grace that I was there and gave God much glory. After the formal meeting, I met Reinhard Bonnke, who laid hands on me and prayed for healing. He also prayed for Rivers. I felt the awesome presence of God that morning, but I knew that this was not my hour for healing. The words kept ringing in my ears, "Two days to revive; third day to restore." Twenty-one days. May 28th was going to be the day.

My physicians advised me to take it easy for a few weeks, and to rest and avoid driving for six months as I had to take seizure medication (just as a precaution). But God was telling me to "Go!" I asked Rivers if she would drive us to Baltimore. I called my friend Bruce Hughes and asked him if there would be any way to get seating at the upcoming Benny Hinn Healing Crusade in Baltimore. I had such a strong unction that if I went to this crusade, God would touch me, as it was taking place on May 28th. Bruce told me that he would have our names added to the list. I informed my church leadership that I was going to the crusade and would be gone for a few days.

Tuesday evening, a few days before the crusade, I received a phone call from a dear friend, Pastor Mark Zehnder, who pastors a large Lutheran church in Omaha, Nebraska. He informed me that our brother, Pastor Greg Smith of St. Louis, Missouri, needed prayer. Greg, a close friend for more than thirty years, had flown into Connecticut the prior week to preach at St. Paul for me while I was hospitalized. After returning to St. Louis, he experienced chest tightness while working in the yard, and because of what had happened to me, he immediately saw his physician for a stress test and an EKG. His physician told him that he had major blockage around his heart and that he must come in the next day—Wednesday, May 26, 2004— for an angiogram. His physician advised Greg that if there

was major blockage, either a stent or bypass surgery would be necessary. Over the phone we prayed for his condition, and I told him that God had his heart in His hand and was healing it, and the doctors would be confounded the next day. Mark and I immediately called Greg and prayed that God would completely restore any damage to his heart and confound the doctors.

The very next day, Rivers and I left for Baltimore. God kept bringing Greg to mind and heart, so en route to Baltimore, I called Greg and left a voice-mail message. God had been creating a great unction for him in me, and I told him so with the specific message that I saw him as "Greg the Lion Hearted" and that he would run with the lions. Later that day, he called and could barely speak. After running the test the first time, the physician told him that he had made a mistake and had to run the test a second time. At the end of the second test, Greg was informed that everything looked great—no blockage was found—and that no further action had to be taken concerning his heart. He was sent home. I told Greg that God had healed him and that he must declare and decree this to his people. Indeed, God would be glorified in this healing, and many of his people, upon hearing his testimony, would be set free. I encouraged my friend to inform his large Lutheran congregation, despite how hard it would be to do so. He agreed in principle and said he would pursue this declaration.

Rivers and I arrived in Baltimore on Wednesday and checked into our hotel. Thursday morning, we met some friends for breakfast and shared a meal of excitement and anticipation. My emotions were mixed: anxious but convicted; hopeful yet scared; questioning myself and yet believing in Jesus. We made our way over to the arena and to our great joy, found ourselves seated five rows from the front. I had a cane and a leg brace (under my trousers), so the thought of a chair in front of me for support was very pacifying. The worship was wonderful, as was every other aspect of the crusade. Unexpectedly, Benny Hinn left the stage and came down the aisle into the crowd. His unplanned sojourn took him directly to us, where he gently prayed for Rivers and me. We both fell back in our seats under the awesome power of the Holy Spirit. God was on the move. After the service, we went back to our room where "Two days to revive; the third day to restore" kept flooding my mind as I drifted into sleep.

The next morning, when we awoke I felt extremely fatigued. I told Rivers that I thought I would rest and not attend the 10:00 A.M. service. She would not hear of this, and she volunteered to go over early and get our seats. I agreed and slowly made my way over about 9:30 A.M. This time we were seated about seven rows back from the front. An event leader came over to us and said that we looked familiar. I mentioned that I was Harald's pastor, and reminded him that we had met the previous August in Madison Square Garden. A few moments later, the man returned and asked us to move to the second row in the middle section. Again he left and again he returned, this time requesting us to follow him to the front row, where he sat us directly in front of the podium! We were shocked, but thrilled. I was feeling a little uncertain about standing for long periods of time (especially directly in front of Benny). A row of chairs in front of me would have been a great security blanket. But God would make a way for me to handle it!

The crusade started. It was a blessed time. Toward the end, Benny called all pastors forward for a blessing. With Rivers's help, I walked to the center of the platform and stood there. Hundreds came for this blessing. As Rivers and I had been blessed by Pastor Benny at the New Jersey and New York City crusades, I was aware of his practice of having some pastors up on stage. I told Rivers that with the leg brace, there was no way I could walk through that crowd and up those stairs. I felt content to just stand there at the base of the stage and wait on the Lord. About that time, a woman came over and told us we had to come on stage to receive a blessing. I told her it was impossible for us to walk up those stairs. She said that we must come, and she led us through a small path security had carved for us. Another man helped me negotiate the steps. Our turn came. Pastor Benny, not once, not twice, but three times, prayed for us. Were we blessed! But I was not healed yet.

We saw the event leader who had helped us in the grill at the hotel that afternoon and thanked him for the premier seating. He apologetically explained that he could not sit us in the front row during the evening service as it was reserved. We thoroughly understood and felt blessed to just to have seating anywhere that was convenient.

Great anticipation surrounded Friday evening. It was Day Twenty-one. Kinglsey's prophecy four years earlier resonated in my heart, mind, and body. Then I realized something significant. The Friday night that Kingsley had given me that word was the Friday evening before Memorial Day 2000. This day was the very same Friday evening before Memorial Day—four years later. "Two days to revive; third day to restore." This was the third Friday since my stroke; the third service at Baltimore. I knew, I knew, I knew that this was the hour God had foretold. Rivers and I were praying with great expectancy!

We made our way over to the arena with brace, cane, and water bottles at about 6:30 P.M. Much to our surprise, we were led to the same two seats in the front that we had sat in the morning service. I asked the woman who had seated us if she had the right people. She said, "The Lord told me to seat you here." A young female pastor who was seated next to me introduced herself. She said that she had been very sick in the restroom in the entrance area and was contemplating leaving before the service began. I told her to stay put, as Satan was trying to rob her of her joy. We prayed for God to intervene and heal her. The service began and about thirty minutes later, she told me that she felt wonderful, and she was delighted that she had stayed. I was selfishly glad that she stayed because I needed Rivers and her to help me stand up.

The flow of the Spirit began to move as soon as we entered into worship. Without warning, I was touched by the power of God. While standing, I began to shake in a way that I cannot duplicate to this day, like a jackhammer that is used to break up concrete. This jerking lasted for about five minutes. Rivers immediately sensed, as I did, that I was being healed. Pastor Benny called out a word of knowledge from the stage that there had been several healings, including someone with a brace. Hallelujah! That was the up side; the down side was that Pastor Benny had demanded that people take off their braces to show it.

The dilemma I now faced was how to deal with that brace under my trousers while I was still standing front and center. For me to take my brace off meant I would have to take my pants off. Right in front of us was the camera on a long boom that moved around the crowd. I certainly could not see myself being caught on national television taking my pants off to remove a leg brace. I did not want to be disobedient, but I really asked the Lord for grace and mercy if I was not complying with His will.

The next thing Pastor Benny did was to call forward those who had experienced a healing. I looked over and saw the multitudes flocking the front stage, eager to share their testimonies. I told myself that Pastor Benny had blessed me several times and that this was their opportunity, not mine. Deep in my mind, I felt like Simon Peter facing that moment when he had to take the step into the Sea of Galilee. I knew that I was healed; I kept shifting my weight back and forth on my legs, but should I go forward to the line? Then I remembered the words of Harald Bredesen: "Make it easy on you and hard on God." That was it! I said, "God, if you want me up on that platform to give witness to what you have done in me, then you make it happen." I felt perfectly safe. My mind started to think about what I would find when I took the brace off in my hotel room. I was ready to go.

All of a sudden, Pastor Benny stopped everything and walked over to the pulpit. He looked directly at Rivers and me and said, "Come up here!" Rivers later reported that she looked around saying, "Do you mean us?" I, on the other hand, was saying to myself, *Well, Lord?* I knew that this command was from God. We walked over to the stairs leading up to the platform. Here was the real test of my healing—the stairs. What moments earlier would have taken me five minutes to ascend, I climbed normally. I knew I was healed! I told a man who was standing at the top of the stairs that God had healed me that very night.

Rivers and I walked toward Pastor Benny. He asked, "Who are you people?" and I said that I was a Lutheran pastor from Westport, Connecticut, and that Harald was my pastor-at-large. He responded, "You are the Lutheran pastor he is always talking about!" Then he asked, "Do Lutherans believe in this?" I said, "This one does." He then touched us and down we went in God's glory. While we were being picked up, Brock told him that I had experienced a miracle. Pastor Benny asked me to share it with the crowd.

I started by sharing about my stroke three weeks earlier and how I felt that I had been healed during worship. Pastor Benny then told us that he had called us onto the platform to proclaim that we were going to have a healing ministry. He prophesied over us these specific and awesome words:

> Stretch your hands toward them that this Sunday miracles would happen in that church.... We believe! As the gospel will be preached out of this man's lips and his wife's, that they'll see mighty signs and wonders as in the Book of Acts. That church will experience such a flow and an overflow and an abundant flow of the Spirit. That Ezekiel 47 will be fulfilled in that congregation where now only their feet are touching the water, but soon that glorious water of life will flow so great and so deep that it will draw thousands into that congregation. Lord, I pray healing ministry would be granted to this couple who've served you for years. Give them that mantle. Touch!

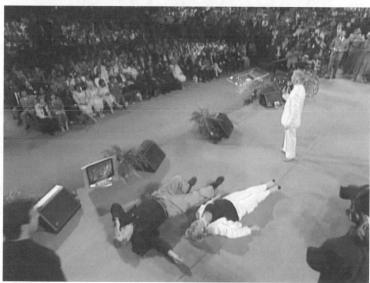

Opposite: Paul and Rivers on the platform with Pastor Benny Hinn, giving testimony of God's healing. Above: Pastor Benny imparts a healing mantle on Paul and Rivers, as they fall under the power of God.

Saturday morning, I awoke up and felt totally restored. While I did not need my brace or my walker, I was still a little weak as we loaded up the car and headed for home. Sunday morning, I told Rivers that I had to go to church to see if people would start coming for healing, as Pastor Benny had said. (I was supposed to be "resting" and was not scheduled to preach for two months.) I attended the second service, sitting in the back of the church. At the beginning of the service, I went forward to assure the people that I was doing well and would return to the pulpit the next Sunday, June 6, which would be the twenty-eighth anniversary of my ordination. I returned to my seat at the rear of the church.

Following the sermon, a lay minister asked for prayer requests. I stood and responded by requesting continued prayers for what God was doing through His people and our church. A woman who had walked into the service late and sat in front of me (she did not hear me speak at the beginning and did not know that I was the pastor) stood up. She said, "God told me that if I came to this church today, I would be healed." She then pointed over her shoulder at me and said, "When I heard that man speak, I knew that I had found the right church." She had traveled approximately thirty miles to our church, and even though she did not know that we existed, she miraculously found St. Paul. Following the service, I went to her and offered to pray for her. While I was praying, she was completely healed. The next morning, she left a message on the church's voice mail saying that the pain she had had for six months was gone and she could now go back to work to a job she had been forced to leave.

As I walked out of that same service, another woman showed me a picture of her grandchild and told me that the little boy (eleven months old) had a blood count of 200 and the doctors thought it was leukemia. I took the picture and prayed that the test results would confound the doctors. She called later that week and told me that the blood count was 720 (a normal count is 1,000) and that the physicians had completely ruled out leukemia. Four weeks later, the blood count was normal, and the physicians said the malady must have been the result of an "unidentifiable virus." They were confounded.

And the flow of miracles did not stop there. A week after I returned from Baltimore, I went to see my physical therapy physician, who examined me thoroughly. He said that I was ahead of where he thought I would be and that within a couple of weeks, I would be out of physical therapy. It took even less time as I quickly maxed out on the exercises. While he was willing to release me, he would only declare me 98 percent functional. (And they had originally told me I would only regain 15 percent!)

My expectation in attending the Benny Hinn crusade was to be fully healed. I had no expectation that Rivers and I would receive a healing mantle. Three weeks after I returned from Baltimore, a staff person from Benny Hinn Ministries called me. She said that she was curious about the prophetic word Pastor Benny had given us. She had reviewed the tape and copied what Pastor Benny said. "I've never seen or heard him speak this way," she told me. I assured her that what he had spoken into us had already started to occur at our church. She sounded encouraged and expressed her joy for us.

Rivers and I were perplexed, yet excitement truly gripped our souls. To God be the glory!

Part Two

8

The Holy Spirit
on the Main Line

In the modern era, several factors are used to measure successful churches: the number of people in worship, the music and programs, the size of the budget, educational opportunities, and the quality of the preaching. The primary focus of most Sunday morning critics is on the message. Why? The twenty-first-century Church is a message-driven Church. But what was the focus of the first-century Church? The first gospel gives us a glimpse of the early Church through the threefold ministry of Jesus, which consisted of teaching, preaching, and healing.

In Matthew, we see an example of His teaching ministry:

> *And Jesus went about all Galilee, **teaching** in their synagogues, **preaching** the gospel of the kingdom, and **healing** all kinds of sickness and all kinds of disease among the people. Then His fame went throughout all Syria; and they brought to Him all sick people who were afflicted with various diseases and torments, and those who were demon-possessed, epileptics, and paralytics; and He healed them. Great multitudes followed Him—from Galilee, and from Decapolis, Jerusalem, Judea, and beyond the Jordan.* (Matthew 4:23-25, boldface mine)

JESUS' TEACHING MINISTRY

Jesus taught extensively on the love of God. In the Sermon on the Mount (see Matthew 5-7), Jesus revealed the depth and breadth of God's will for us to love Him and others. He took religious standards under the Law to a higher level under grace. Adultery was not just a sexual act, but an attitude of the heart that permeated the whole man. Murder was not just the taking of a physical life, but the malice and hatred that desired death for another person.

Why was Jesus' teaching so life giving? So startling? Throughout history, for generations after generations, the Pharisees had taken the Decalogue and extrapolated 613 rules from it. Forty percent of the rules were positive and the other 60 percent were negative. Saving grace from sin, as identified by the Law, was nonexistent. When questioned by the Pharisees as to which commandment was the greatest, Jesus responded with wisdom beyond comprehension and said that the first and greatest commandment was to love God. Secondly, but no less important, was the command to love each other.

> *But when the Pharisees heard that He had silenced the Sadducees, they gathered together. Then one of them, a lawyer, asked Him a question, testing Him, and saying, "Teacher, which is the great commandment in the law?" Jesus said to him, "'You shall love the LORD your God with all your heart, with all your soul, and with all your mind.' This is the first and great commandment. And the second is like it: 'You shall love your neighbor as yourself.' On these two commandments hang all the Law and the Prophets." (Matthew 22:34-40)*

Jesus instructed that we must have a vertical relationship with God (see John 3) and a horizontal relationship with others that reflects our love for God. (See Matthew 25.) One without the other is meaningless.

He also taught the difference between being "right" and "righteous." In John 8, a woman was brought to Jesus who had been caught in the act of adultery. The religious leaders, seeking to trap Jesus, asked Him if she should be put to death by stoning, which was the expected response under the Law of Moses. Jesus did not choose the "right" thing, but the "righteous" thing. He had every right under the Law of Moses to have her stoned, but He chose to forgive and release her. Righteousness over rightness was both His wisdom and His heart.

Teaching was an integral part of Jesus' ministry. And it was a nonstop ministry. Everywhere He went, He taught. His most unique peripatetic teaching style, which was teaching as He walked using His environment as His classroom, opened the eyes of His followers about the end times, the second judgment, and many other subjects concerning life in the Kingdom.

JESUS' PREACHING MINISTRY

Teaching in love, Jesus also preached the arrival of the long-awaited Jewish Messiah—the Good News. His preaching style was didactic and resolute. He *was* the Messiah. Israel had been expecting a messianic figure from the time of proclamation found in Deuteronomy 18:15: *"The LORD your God will raise up for you a prophet."* However, over the centuries, messianic figures had come and gone, but none had met the test. Jesus, while preaching in the synagogue in Nazareth, made the claim that he was the Messiah, as we see in Luke 4:

> *So He came to Nazareth, where He had been brought up. And as His custom was, He went into the synagogue on the Sabbath day, and stood up to read. And He was handed the book of the prophet Isaiah. And when He had opened the book, He found the place where it was written:*

> *The Spirit of the LORD is upon Me,*
> *Because He has anointed Me*
> *To preach the gospel to the poor;*
> *He has sent Me to heal the brokenhearted,*
> *To proclaim liberty to the captives*
> *And recovery of sight to the blind,*
> *To set at liberty those who are oppressed;*
> *To proclaim the acceptable year of the LORD.*

> *Then He closed the book, and gave it back to the attendant and sat down. And the eyes of all who were in the synagogue were fixed on Him. And He began to say to them, "Today this Scripture is fulfilled in your hearing." (Luke 4:16-21)*

Biblically speaking, there are two types of people in the world—Jews and Gentiles. People are not born Christian or Hindu or Buddhist or Islamic; they are born Gentile. In the context of their environment, they become religious. Gentiles can evolve as followers of any number of world religions depending upon their cultural influences. Jews usually follow the religion of Judaism, but they can also choose to be secular, atheistic, or even messianic believers.

In either case, Jews and Gentiles are products of their respective cultures.

If Jesus is the long-awaited Jewish Messiah, then it is imperative that all people, both Jews and Gentiles, believe in Him as the Lamb of God who takes away the sin of the world. The redemptive work of Jesus on the Cross provides the only way back to the Father, and the Resurrection provides hope to a hopeless world. This is the message of the gospel that Jesus preached. To confirm Jesus' claim, the heavenly Father allowed Him to perform miracles, which included healing and deliverance.

JESUS' HEALING MINISTRY

Jesus did not just teach and preach as He moved throughout the region of the Jordan. Jesus also healed and delivered many people. Matthew records that people flocked to Jesus for healing. They did not come to Jesus bearing "notebooks" to hear and record his words of wisdom; they came in great numbers to be healed and delivered. Jesus had a healing ministry.

In Peter's sermon to the household of Cornelius, he states that God anointed Jesus of Nazareth with the Holy Spirit and with power, and then He came out of the river doing good and healing all who were oppressed by the devil because God was with Him, as revealed in Acts 10:

> *... that word you know, which was proclaimed throughout all Judea, and began from Galilee after the baptism which John preached: how God anointed Jesus of Nazareth with the Holy Spirit and with power, who went about doing good and*

healing all who were oppressed by the devil, for God was with Him. And we are witnesses of all things which He did both in the land of the Jews and in Jerusalem, whom they killed by hanging on a tree. (Acts 10:37-39)

Luke 4 records the progression of events as Jesus began His ministry. First, Jesus was baptized in the Jordan, where God sent the Holy Spirit in power and verbally commissioned Jesus for His ministry. Then the Spirit led Jesus into the wilderness, where He was tempted by the enemy. After this, Jesus began His ministry in power. As clearly indicated by the synoptic gospels, Jesus began from this point forward to heal and deliver those who were oppressed by demons.

The gospels are full of accounts in which Jesus healed and moved in deliverance. Furthermore, He did not reserve the right of healing just for himself, but He imparted it to His disciples. In Luke 9, Jesus sent out the twelve, giving them power and authority over all demons to cure diseases and to preach the Kingdom of God and to heal the sick. And they, too, moved in power.

Then, in Luke 10, Jesus sent out the seventy disciples. In verses 5 through 11, Jesus gave them these instructions:

"But whatever house you enter, first say, 'Peace to this house.' And if a son of peace is there, your peace will rest on it; if not, it will return to you. And remain in the same house, eating and drinking such things as they give, for the laborer is worthy of his wages. Do not go from house to house. Whatever city you enter, and they receive you, eat such things as

*are set before you. And heal the sick there, and say to
them, 'The kingdom of God has come near to you.'
But whatever city you enter, and they do not receive
you, go out into its streets and say, 'The very dust of
your city which clings to us we wipe off against you.
Nevertheless know this, that the kingdom of God
has come near you.'"* (Luke 10:5-11)

First they were to declare peace as they approached a
home. If the peace was received, then they were to enter
into the house. If the people rejected the peace, they moved
on. If the host invited them into the home, they initiated
step two: They broke bread. Eating is a time of fellowship
where relationships are built and trust is established. Third,
the two travelers offered to pray for the sick, to release
the power of God to heal the sick and deliver them from
demons. The final step focused on sharing the Good News
of the Kingdom of God. Assuming that once the power of
God touched their lives, those seeing the demonstration
of the power of God would be open to hear and receive
the message about the source of their power. Indeed, the
seventy returned in joy and exuberance, declaring that even
the demons were subject to them in the name of Jesus.

Over and over again Jesus exhorted His own to follow
Him in miraculous action. In John 14, 15, and 16, Jesus
explained to His followers that the Holy Spirit was coming
to guide them; that He would open their ears to hear the
voice of the Father; and that He would give them their
marching orders. The Holy Spirit would empower them
to do even greater miracles than they had witnessed in
His own life. In short, the Church would move forward

demonstrating the triumphant power of Jesus to win the lost for the Kingdom.

Jesus clearly directed His Church to go forth in power in Mark 16, setting New Testament expectations for the Body of Christ. This text reveals that Jesus appeared to the disciples as they were eating and rebuked their unbelief and hardness of heart, because they did not believe those who had seen Him after He had risen. He then told them to go into the world and preach the gospel. This commissioning was personal, for He told them that anyone who believed in Him would cast out demons, speak with new tongues, and lay hands on the sick for healing. Jesus clearly intended the early Church to actively engage in teaching, preaching, and healing.

> *And He said to them, "Go into all the world and preach the gospel to every creature. He who believes and is baptized will be saved; but he who does not believe will be condemned. And these signs will follow those who believe: In My name they will cast out demons; they will speak with new tongues; they will take up serpents; and if they drink anything deadly, it will by no means hurt them; they will lay hands on the sick, and they will recover." So then, after the Lord had spoken to them, He was received up into heaven, and sat down at the right hand of God. And they went out and preached everywhere, the Lord working with them and confirming the word through the accompanying signs. Amen.* (Mark 16:15-20)

9

Whom Did Jesus Heal?

A magnificent blessing of the gospels is that they give us a powerful understanding of how Jesus responded to people who sought Him for healing and deliverance. Whom did Jesus heal? The Scriptures answer this question, and its answer is validated today by actual healing accounts.

Faith seems to play an important role in healing. The range of faith includes those with strong amounts to those with seemingly no faith whatsoever. The following are biblical narratives of those whom Jesus healed as well as actual contemporary examples from my ministry.

STRONG FAITH

Jesus healed several people based on their strong faith, including the following excellent example from Matthew 15:

> Then Jesus went out from there and departed to the region of Tyre and Sidon. And behold, a woman of Canaan came from that region and cried out to Him, saying, "Have mercy on me, O Lord, Son of David! My daughter is severely demon-possessed." But He answered her not a word. And His disciples came and urged Him, saying, "Send her away, for she cries out after us." But He answered and said, "I

was not sent except to the lost sheep of the house of Israel." Then she came and worshiped Him, saying, "Lord, help me!" But He answered and said, "It is not good to take the children's bread and throw it to the little dogs." And she said, "Yes, Lord, yet even the little dogs eat the crumbs which fall from their masters' table." Then Jesus answered and said to her, "O woman, great is your faith! Let it be to you as you desire." And her daughter was healed from that very hour. (Matthew 15:21-28)

In the spring of 2005, Gregg Healey, a young, thirty-five-year-old elder of St. Paul, had a slipped disc that bulged and put pressure on a nerve in his lower back. The pressure eventually resulted in a loss of sensation in his left leg and foot. Because of this pressure, he developed a "foot drop" requiring a brace to keep his foot from drooping and causing him to stumble. A neurosurgeon determined that Gregg would need surgery to correct his back. A man of strong faith, Gregg took the situation to God in prayer. Because Gregg was willing to do anything God wanted him to do, God spoke to Gregg and told him that on a certain date in June, he would be healed. He believed he had definitely heard from God; he was convinced beyond a doubt that God was going to heal him.

Gregg was also planning to go with me to Africa in June, so at the advice of the surgeon, he had his surgery several weeks before our June departure. The surgery was successful, and his back ailment was corrected, as was his leg and foot. Very quickly, Gregg was fully restored. Though puzzled by his need for surgery, he still believed that a "healing" was coming later in June. He waited obediently for the Lord to act.

While we were in South Africa, Gregg had two dreams about his father. These dreams took place on the very date God had given him for his healing, and they revealed to Gregg that he had in his heart some unresolved issues causing negative feelings about his father. The existence of these issues and their resultant negative feelings needed to be healed. The revelatory nature of the dreams was so clear that Gregg knew he had work to do with his father. He immediately called his father from our camp in Africa and the deep-seated issues that he had inadvertently lodged in his heart against his father were released to God. His heart was healed. The relationship with his father was healed. God honored the date that He had given Gregg for healing.

Gregg's strong faith rested in the fact that God was going to heal him on the date that had been given to him from God. At first, he assumed the healing was related to his back problem, but when he actually had to have surgery to correct his bulging disc, his faith never wavered. He knew that God had spoken to him and that healing was en route to him on a specific date in June. He did not know what or how, but he strongly clung to his hope for healing—in one way or another. The healing he received in his relationship with his father was far more important than the healing of his back.

When we are unable to see the plans of God clearly, the testimony of Gregg's strong faith bears witness to the need to trust God, believing that He will honor His word and bring to fruition the promises He makes to us. God will make a way. We must trust God no matter what the circumstance. As Isaiah 32:17 tells us: *"The work of righteousness will be peace. And the effect of righteousness, quietness and assurance forever."*

NORMAL FAITH

Some people whom Jesus healed seemed to have a "normal" dose of faith. They trusted Jesus and simply responded to His healing touch, as seen in the healing of Peter's mother-in-law in Matthew 8:

> *Now when Jesus had come into Peter's house, He saw his wife's mother lying sick with a fever. So He touched her hand, and the fever left her. And she arose and served them. When evening had come, they brought to Him many who were demon-possessed. And He cast out the spirits with a word, and healed all who were sick, that it might be fulfilled which was spoken by Isaiah the prophet, saying: "He Himself took our infirmities and bore our sicknesses."* (Matthew 8:14-17)

A man came to me following a service and asked me to pray for him. He had contracted Lyme disease and was undergoing major treatment to hold the disease in check. The disease, which attacks the joints and nervous system, had left him marginally debilitated. He was desperate, but hoping that God would heal him. He told me that he was Roman Catholic and believed that with God, all things were possible. I anointed him with oil and placed my hands on him. I had him pray asking God to heal him; then I declared to him that God had healed him. As I looked into his eyes, God gave me a word of knowledge for him. I proceeded to tell him the name of the doctor who was treating him. His eyes widened and he exclaimed, "How did you know that?" I said God had revealed it to me as a sign to him that God had healed him of Lyme disease. He later reported to me that God had, indeed, healed him of the disease. Because of this encounter, his faith went to the next level!

WEAK FAITH

Jesus did not restrict His healing to those with great or normal faith. He sometimes responded to weak faith, as we see in the story of the man who brought his young son to the disciples.

> And when He came to the disciples, He saw a great multitude around them, and scribes disputing with them. Immediately, when they saw Him, all the people were greatly amazed, and running to Him, greeted Him. And He asked the scribes, "What are you discussing with them?" Then one of the crowd answered and said, "Teacher, I brought You my son, who has a mute spirit. And wherever it seizes him, it throws him down; he foams at the mouth, gnashes his teeth, and becomes rigid. So I spoke to Your disciples, that they should cast it out, but they could not."
>
> He answered him and said, "O faithless generation, how long shall I be with you? How long shall I bear with you? Bring him to Me." Then they brought him to Him. And when he saw Him, immediately the spirit convulsed him, and he fell on the ground and wallowed, foaming at the mouth.
>
> So He asked his father, "How long has this been happening to him?" And he said, "From childhood. And often he has thrown him both into the fire and into the water to destroy him. But if You can do anything, have compassion on us and help us." Jesus said to him, "If you can believe, all things are

possible to him who believes." Immediately the
father of the child cried out and said with tears,
"Lord, I believe; help my unbelief!" When Jesus saw
that the people came running together, He rebuked
the unclean spirit, saying to it, "Deaf and dumb
spirit, I command you, come out of him and enter
him no more!" Then the spirit cried out, convulsed
him greatly, and came out of him. And he became
as one dead, so that many said, "He is dead." But
Jesus took him by the hand and lifted him up, and
he arose. (Mark 9:14-27)

Rivers and I were invited to share our healing ministry
with the leadership of a nonprofit organization in a major
East Coast city. The forty-five minutes we were initially
allotted to speak turned into two-and-a-half hours as the
mostly evangelical businessmen and women asked several
questions. They seemed quite open to what God was doing
in our lives through our ministry.

At the end of our meeting, one of the men asked me if I
would pray for a young secretary who had a problem with
her leg. I agreed and he ushered me into a small office. He
introduced a young woman to me who wore a black Velcro
cast on her leg that went up to the bottom of her knee. I
asked her to tell me what she needed prayer for and she
shared that she had torn her Achilles tendon and was facing
the possibility of surgery. She seemed nervous but open
to prayer. I asked her if Rivers and I could pray that God
would heal her and she said, "Yes." After saying a healing
prayer, I asked her if she would like to take off her cast. She
declined. I encouraged her to take the cast off after she got
home to see how her leg was and she agreed.

I never want to be presumptuous or tell the Lord what to do, but during the night, I asked God to use this healing as a sign to the evangelical men and women. I asked that He show himself as the God of yesterday who is still alive and well, and healing today.

The next morning, Rivers and I went to see the woman in her office. The first thing we noticed was that she was wearing two shoes. The cast was gone! With tears in her eyes, she told us that her leg was completely healed, and then she said something that only a woman would truly understand. She said that she had been asked to be a bridesmaid in a wedding in two weeks. She knew that if she had the surgery, she could not participate. But if she did not have the operation, she would still have to wear the boot cast for support and also could not be in the wedding. As of this day, she could be in that wedding. She was elated that God had healed her.

The news of her healing spread quickly and was "cause" for those who knew her story to confess that God still heals today!

A woman came to a midweek healing service out of desperation. Her breast cancer had metastasized throughout her body, and her physician had told her that there was nothing further the medical community could do for her. However, her cardiologist told her that there was a church in Westport, Connecticut, that held healing services. The cancer-laden woman began to investigate the churches in Westport and eventually she turned up at St. Paul on a Wednesday night. I will never forget what she first said to me when we met: "I am Lutheran and did not know that Lutherans did this sort of thing." I explained our ministry and what God

was doing through my wife and me. She was encouraged, but very doubtful that anything was going to work.

Within six weeks, she was cancer-free. She was both elated and amazed. She continued to attend, but over time she began to doubt her healing. She intellectually understood the nature of her disease and believed it was a only matter of time before the cancer returned. Approximately three months later, she reported that she had three tumors in her brain. I continued to pray for her and told her to believe God—for the present and the future. He would heal her brain. The tumors in her brain did leave, and she was cancer-free again. But she needed more intellectual proof. Her mind and faith were in conflict. But our God is merciful and patient and kind. She went in for a full-body PET scan, which revealed that she had absolutely no tumors or cancer in her body. Hallelujah!

THE FAITH OF OTHERS

In a few biblical examples, Jesus responded to the faith of those who were bringing people to Him for healing, rather than the faith of the sick people themselves. An excellent example is found in Matthew 8:

> *Now when Jesus had entered Capernaum, a centurion came to Him, pleading with Him, saying, "Lord, my servant is lying at home paralyzed, dreadfully tormented." And Jesus said to him, "I will come and heal him." The centurion answered and said, "Lord, I am not worthy that You should come under my roof. But only speak a word, and my servant will be healed. For I also am a man under authority, having soldiers under me. And I say to*

this one, 'Go,' and he goes; and to another, 'Come,' and he comes; and to my servant, 'Do this,' and he does it." When Jesus heard it, He marveled, and said to those who followed, "Assuredly, I say to you, I have not found such great faith, not even in Israel! And I say to you that many will come from east and west, and sit down with Abraham, Isaac, and Jacob in the kingdom of heaven. But the sons of the kingdom will be cast out into outer darkness. There will be weeping and gnashing of teeth." Then Jesus said to the centurion, "Go your way; and as you have believed, so let it be done for you." And his servant was healed that same hour. (Matthew 8:5-13)

I received a call from a businessman in the Baltimore area who told me that his brother was in a coma in a West Coast hospital after having had a stroke. The family was facing the painful decision of whether or not to turn off the life-support system that was sustaining him. I asked if there was any brain activity and my friend answered in the affirmative. "What do you believe you should do?" I asked him. He said to pray that God would heal him. He had the faith. We prayed together over the phone that his brother would, indeed, be healed. The next day, his brother came out of the coma and within a few days went home to his wife and family.

While in China praying and ministering, two women checked a friend out of the hospital and brought her to our prayer meeting. She was young and paralyzed from the waist down due to her spine being severed in an automobile accident a few months earlier. As they carried her across the room, they literally cradled her under their arms and carried her toward the stage with her lifeless legs hanging limp—the tips of her toes were dragging across the cement floor. I prayed for the stripes of Jesus to be wrapped around her body and for healing to be released into her spine. Within minutes, she was standing on her own. Then she started to take steps, weak and wobbly, but she walked on her own weight. Her friends could not contain themselves. Neither could anyone else in the room. Explosion erupted. Their applause must have reached Heaven that night. God is awesome!

No Faith

Jesus even healed those who were hopeless in their quest for healing. The man at the pool of Bethesda had no expectancy for healing, yet Jesus' healing touch came in spite of it.

> *After this there was a feast of the Jews, and Jesus went up to Jerusalem. Now there is in Jerusalem by the Sheep Gate a pool, which is called in Hebrew, Bethesda, having five porches. In these lay a great multitude of sick people, blind, lame, paralyzed, waiting for the moving of the water. For an angel went down at a certain time into the pool and stirred up the water; then whoever stepped in first, after the stirring of the water, was made well of whatever disease he had. Now a certain man was there who had an infirmity thirty-eight years. When Jesus saw him lying there, and knew that he already had been in that condition a long time, He said to him, "Do you want to be made well?" The sick man answered Him, "Sir, I have no man to put me into the pool*

when the water is stirred up; but while I am coming, another steps down before me." Jesus said to him, "Rise, take up your bed and walk." And immediately the man was made well, took up his bed, and walked. And that day was the Sabbath. (John 5:1-9)

One Wednesday night, a young woman whom I did not know came for prayer. Rivers was with me that night, and we both heard her story of how she was scheduled for surgery for cervical cancer the following week. I asked her how she heard about our church and she answered that a girlfriend had told her about a healing church in Westport. She lived about twenty miles away and decided to "find" that church and come for prayer. I asked her if she attended church and she said no. I then asked her if she was a follower of Jesus and she again said no. Here was a moment ripe for a miracle. I told her that Jesus was going to heal her to show her how much He loved her, and I anointed her with oil and placed my hands on her head. I declared the cancer null and void and pronounced her healed in the name of Jesus. She slowly fell backward to the floor under the presence of the Spirit. Rivers and another prayer team member began to pray over her. The woman eventually stood up and left. Later, Rivers reported that while they had been praying over the young woman, she had smelled an odor that was putrid and rank. Rivers said it was horrible, but had soon dissipated after prayer.

A week later, the woman returned to report that she had asked the physician to examine her one more time before the scheduled surgery. He agreed and discovered that the cancer was completely gone. I asked her if she was ready to accept Jesus as her Lord and Savior, but she said she could not. Her father had done something to violate her trust and as a result, she had turned her back on the Lord. Yet she continued to attend our healing services. After several months of encouraging her to receive Jesus, she finally said that she could not believe in God and left our church.

About two years later, she returned to the church for more healing prayer because symptoms of the cancer were starting to return. I asked her if she wanted a relationship with the Jesus who had healed her originally and who continued to love her. Again she said no to the offer of salvation. She only wanted healing prayer. I explained to her that Jesus had revealed His power once and wanted to fill her with His love. I told her that I believed God had opened a window for her through healing, but now that window was closing. Jesus had demonstrated His great love for her with the first healing and wanted to be fully part of her life. She looked at me and said that she could not accept Jesus or God into her life. She left and I never saw her again. I believe that as broken as my heart was for her, God's heart was broken even more.

I must point out that a lack of faith can even tie the hands of Jesus and prevent Him from healing, as recorded in Mark 6:

> *Then He went out from there and came to His own country, and His disciples followed Him. And when the Sabbath had come, He began to teach in the synagogue. And many hearing Him were astonished, saying, "Where did this Man get these things? And what wisdom is this which is given to Him, that such mighty works are performed by His*

hands! Is this not the carpenter, the Son of Mary, and brother of James, Joses, Judas, and Simon? And are not His sisters here with us?" So they were offended at Him. But Jesus said to them, "A prophet is not without honor except in his own country, among his own relatives, and in his own house." Now He could do no mighty work there, except that He laid His hands on a few sick people and healed them. And He marveled because of their unbelief. Then He went about the villages in a circuit, teaching. (Mark 6:1-6)

I have been in meetings where the bar of faith has been flat and as a result, the move of God was stymied and people were not healed. In one such meeting, a man came up to me to tell me that he did not believe in today's healing ministries. My response was simple: If he did not believe in healing then he could just stay sick. He challenged me by responding, "Are you saying that I do not have faith to be healed?" "No," I continued, "I am simply agreeing with you that if you do not believe in healing, then *you* are saying in essence that *you* do not have faith." I have learned that if a person is not open to signs, wonders, and miracles, then short of a major personal miracle, they will not open up. Arguing is not going to persuade them.

Do you not believe that I am in the Father, and the Father in Me? The words that I speak to you I do not speak on My own authority; but the Father who dwells in Me does the works. Believe Me that I am in the Father and the Father in Me, or else believe Me for the sake of the works themselves. (John 14:10-11)

When Healing Doesn't Happen

It is always a joy to watch God's healing touch. But sometimes in my ministry, I have to watch the absence of obvious physical healing. Faith could be there. Compassion could be there. Desire could be there. But healing was not. In these situations I have to remind myself that I do not understand the mind of God. Sometimes He heals and sometimes He does not heal.

> *Then He spoke a parable to them, that men always ought to pray and not lose heart, saying: "There was in a certain city a judge who did not fear God nor regard man. Now there was a widow in that city; and she came to him, saying, 'Get justice for me from my adversary.' And he would not for a while; but afterward he said within himself, 'Though I do not fear God nor regard man, yet because this widow troubles me I will avenge her, lest by her continual coming she weary me.'" Then the Lord said, "Hear what the unjust judge said. And shall God not avenge His own elect who cry out day and night to Him, though He bears long with them? I tell you that He will avenge them speedily. Nevertheless, when the Son of Man comes, will He really find faith on the earth?" (Luke 18:1-8)*

This parable in Luke teaches us much about overcoming. Overcoming is very important when healing is not at first evident. In Luke 18 Jesus is encouraging us to pray, pray, pray! Do not throw in the towel! Press in to God with prayer and do not lose heart!

Jesus is looking for people of faith who will trust Him. We must acknowledge that God is good! He knows what He is doing, and we can trust Him. If we remind ourselves of these undeniable, unshakeable, unflappable character traits of God, He will make a way. My motto is: Anything this side of the grave is manageable! What greater testimony to our faith than the profession we make through Matthew 19:26: *"But Jesus looked at them and said to them, 'With men this is impossible, but with God all things are possible.'"*

A WORD OF WARNING

We must be careful not to denounce healing and deliverance today. While Jesus was casting out demons by the power of the Spirit, He came under attack by the religious leaders. Listen to how Jesus responded to their argument that He was casting out demons by the power of Beelzebub, the ruler of the demons, in Matthew 12:

> *Then one was brought to Him who was demon-possessed, blind and mute; and He healed him, so that the blind and mute man both spoke and saw. And all the multitudes were amazed and said, "Could this be the Son of David?" Now when the Pharisees heard it they said, "This fellow does not cast out demons except by Beelzebub, the ruler of the demons." But Jesus knew their thoughts, and said to them: "Every kingdom divided against itself is brought to desolation, and every city or house divided against itself will not stand. If Satan casts out Satan, he is divided against himself. How then will his kingdom stand? And if I cast out demons by Beelzebub, by whom do your sons cast them out?*

Therefore they shall be your judges. But if I cast out demons by the Spirit of God, surely the kingdom of God has come upon you. Or how can one enter a strong man's house and plunder his goods, unless he first binds the strong man? And then he will plunder his house. He who is not with Me is against Me, and he who does not gather with Me scatters abroad. Therefore I say to you, every sin and blasphemy will be forgiven men, but the blasphemy against the Spirit will not be forgiven men. Anyone who speaks a word against the Son of Man, it will be forgiven him; but whoever speaks against the Holy Spirit, it will not be forgiven him, either in this age or in the age to come. " (Matthew 12:22-32)

Here is the ever-present danger: Jesus says that you can be forgiven if you blaspheme Him, but not if you blaspheme the work of the Holy Spirit. Why? Because the Spirit of God can be grieved and then He retreats. If the Spirit leaves, then we are not able to confess Jesus Christ as Lord:

"Therefore I make known to you that no one speaking by the Spirit of God calls Jesus accursed, and no one can say that Jesus is Lord except by the Holy Spirit" (1 Corinthians 12:3).

I served as a navy chaplain for twenty years. I frequently heard God's name and the name of Jesus used in vain or in thoughtless profanity. But I cannot once remember hearing a person use the name of the Holy Spirit in a profane way. Could God be protecting humanity in an innate way from abusing the name of the Holy Spirit? Interesting.

In addition to faith, Jesus had many other reasons for healing.

10

Why Did Jesus Heal?

THE REASON OF COMPASSION

God is compassionate, and this characteristic is showcased in the Scriptures in five distinct healing experiences. Jesus was moved deeply by the desperation of those who came to Him seeking His restorative touch, as reflected in Matthew 14:

> *When Jesus heard it, He departed from there by boat to a deserted place by Himself. But when the multitudes heard it, they followed Him on foot from the cities. And when Jesus went out He saw a great multitude; and He was moved with compassion for them, and healed their sick.* (Matthew 14:13-14)

An elderly woman was sitting in church one night at a healing service. She suffered with carpal tunnel syndrome and arthritis in both hands. As the praise worship filled the room, she began to feel heat flowing down her arms and into both hands. Heat radiated to her fingertips. All of a sudden, she felt the pain in her hands disappear. She sat with her family, saying nothing out loud, instead, silently thanking God for the unrequested gift of healing. The service concluded, and as she passed by me at the back of the sanctuary, I noticed tears on her face. I asked the daughter what had happened and she said she did not know.

The next week, they returned. I again inquired about her tears, but this time I was told about the healing of her hands. I asked her if she would give her testimony to build faith in the room, which she did with great joy and enthusiasm. Our God of great mercy had seen her in the pews, and His compassion was moved to heal her then and there.

Another wonderful healing of compassion occurred in 2002 at a local pediatric critical care unit. Late one evening, a frantic mother called me to come to the hospital. When I arrived, I found the father and mother standing by a hospital crib with a clear plastic tent over their four-week-old infant son. He was pale and barely breathing. The local hospital staff had called a pediatric hospital thirty miles away to transport the baby to its better-equipped facility.

God then moved me to do something highly unusual. I placed my hand under the plastic tent and lightly touched the baby's chest. In faith, I told the father that God was healing his infant son to let him know his heavenly Father loved him and his family. I said, "As much as you love your son—God loves you more."

The pediatric critical care hospital staff arrived to transport the baby. A physician and nurse from the new hospital began to examine the child. The doctor looked at the X-rays, then went back to the child for another check of his health. He seemed perplexed and asked the local nurses why he had even been called. I heard the doctor say that the baby's color was good and his lungs were clear because he was able to feed on a bottle. The local nurses continued to state that the child had exhibited serious symptoms. Since the pediatric ICU team had driven a long distance, they agreed to take the baby back to their hospital for observation. But because he no longer exhibited symptoms, their recommendation would be to place him in general—not ICU—care.

The very next day, the mother called me and said that the child had been discharged and was at home healthy and doing well. She was humble and, of course, thankful for the miracle. I encouraged them to come to church weekly to give God the glory and, indeed, they did!

THE REASON TO GLORIFY GOD

God, and God alone, must receive all the glory and honor and praise and thanks. One joyous reason Jesus healed was to bring glory to His Father in Heaven, as alluded to in John 9:

> *Now as Jesus passed by, He saw a man who was blind from birth. And His disciples asked Him, saying, "Rabbi, who sinned, this man or his parents, that he was born blind?" Jesus answered, "Neither this man nor his parents sinned, but that the works of God should be revealed in him. I must work the works of Him who sent Me while it is day; the night is coming when no one can work. As long as I am in the world, I am the light of the world." When He had said these things, He spat on the ground and made clay with the saliva; and He anointed the eyes of the blind man with the clay. And He said to him, "Go, wash in the pool of Siloam" (which is translated, Sent). So he went and washed, and came back seeing. (John 9:1-7)*

One Sunday in June 2009, a father brought his twelve-year-old daughter, Emma, up for prayer at the end of the Sunday morning service. He told me that a small lump had been discovered on his daughter's shoulder. The pediatricians ordered a biopsy, which determined that it was a rare cancer that only a handful of children develop each year. Furthermore, the prognosis was hopeless. They were told by the physicians that they had never seen this type of cancer cured. Rivers and I took the lead to have St. Paul Westport begin to pray for God to intervene and heal Emma. One day while we were visiting her in the hospital, I told the dad that God was going to heal his daughter and that he would stand in front of the congregation and give his testimony.

In August 2009, my twelve-year-old grandson, Tyler, heard God speak to him on a Monday night telling him that a young child in the church was going to be healed. While driving to the Wednesday night healing service two days later to pray for the child, Tyler asked me if Emma ever came on Wednesday nights to the healing service. I told him she had never come to a healing and deliverance service. As the worship began, Emma walked in with her father. After a time of praise, I invited the children to come forward with their parents for healing prayer. I instructed Tyler to anoint them with oil, lay hands on them, and declare healing over their lives by the stripes of Jesus. (For five years, Rivers and I have taken Tyler with us on missionary trips to Scandinavia, the United Kingdom, Africa, and Canada. He has witnessed many miracles, signs, and wonders.) The net result of all these prayers would soon be revealed.

On Sunday, October 16, 2009, the congregation celebrated my twenty-year anniversary at St. Paul. I had a young evangelist, Michael Koulianos, speak that morning. While he and I stood together in the front of the church at the end of the service, Emma ran down the center aisle with a handful of cards the children's church had made for Rivers and me. Michael inquired as to why she was wearing a stocking cap, and I told him that we were praying for her healing. He asked if we could pray for her right then and there. I told the entire church to stretch out their hands toward Emma, and Michael declared her healed in the name of Jesus. The entire congregation wholeheartedly agreed with a loud "Amen."

As Emma's father came through the communion line the following Sunday, he told me that the oncologist at Yale Medical Center had run a series of tests and could find no cancer in Emma. I asked him to share this report to the congregation at the end of the service. When he shared the awesome news, the church erupted into pandemonium. People were shouting and praising God as one voice. Waves of enthusiasm rolled across the sanctuary. The noise would start to subside, but then the roar of the saints would explode again. That morning was one of the most extraordinary we had ever experienced. (Rivers later shared that people in the past had shown excitement for healing that had occurred at St. Paul, but this day was like no other.) After five minutes or so, I announced that there was "an atmosphere for healing in the house." If anyone wanted healing prayer, they should come forward. People ran to the front. God touched many people that morning.

Much to our surprise, God revealed His presence by allowing *gold dust* to cover one of the pews. People who had left the service to go into the fellowship room streamed back in to see this wonderful manifestation of His glory. As the Bible says, we cannot see God face-to-face, but we can behold His glory. Without reservation, this experience was a pivotal moment for St. Paul Westport—a pre-Epiphany Epiphany! God healed to reveal His *glory*!

I believe the best way to share Emma's healing is through the words of her dad:

On June 26, 2009, my daughter Emma, twelve years old then, had a routine operation to remove a lump on her left shoulder at Yale-New Haven Children's Hospital. Otherwise, Emma seemed perfectly healthy. She is so young and talented at so many things that it did not seem like anything bad was going to happen. Five pediatricians and two surgeons were comfortable that the lump was nothing to worry about. None were concerned. But after the surgery, the biopsy determined it was cancer. Pathology and imaging showed it to be "high grade pleomorphic undifferentiated sarcoma," which her oncologist was sure had metastasized to her lungs in several small but measurable nodules. The number of mitotic figures on the slides was extremely high, meaning that this was a very aggressive, fast-growing cancer.

We learned that this is such a rare form of cancer that only a handful of children get it each year. We learned that this means that no one knows what treatment, or whether any treatment, will work against it. One of the surgeons at Yale who treated Emma concluded that "no chemo or radiation therapy has been shown to be effective" against this cancer. He repeated this three times, each time taking us to a new low. The pediatric oncologist at Yale wrote that he had informed my wife and I of the prognosis, which had left us with horrible fear that Emma would not be with us much longer, "but they both feel that we need to give Emma this intensive chemotherapy and radiation therapy." The doctors provided little hope, although they assured us that they would do everything medically possible to help Emma. The same news came from Memorial Sloan-Kettering and Columbia University in New York City.

We started an extreme course of chemo and radiation therapy over a six-month period, with hospitalization every third week. Many people seemed to come out of nowhere to help us. Friends brought meals; friends and family traveled to help watch Emma's sisters. Friends and family from places in Pennsylvania, Delaware, Maryland, Michigan, Georgia, and more were hoping and praying.

One place I turned to was St. Paul's Lutheran Church in Westport, Connecticut. We had started going there about two years before all of this happened. I had felt drawn to this church, believing it was time that my daughters learned more about God and the Bible in Sunday school. I had also been raised in a traditional Lutheran household, where my grandfather and several uncles and cousins were Lutheran ministers, so St. Paul's seemed to be a natural choice.

St. Paul's was very different for me. When I was younger, we never strayed from what I remember as a red hymnal. While every service was the same according to the calendar, and thus comfortable, God felt very abstract. I do not remember any discussion of healing with the Holy Spirit in either church or our home. The name of Jesus was spoken, of course, but not so much in adoration. In contrast, St.

Paul's describes itself as an Antioch church, and it seemed to be modeled on many of the passages in the New Testament where Jesus is in people's lives day by day and minute by minute, not just on Sunday.

That red hymnal I remember is not followed at the later service when Sunday school is offered, although I doubt now whether there is anything like the red hymnal anymore. Instead, the service has a highly skilled rock-type band with electric guitars and drum sets. A large screen projection TV displays the words of the contemporary songs that are sung, as well as the points made in the sermons. But you could never say that God is an abstract concept here: The Holy Spirit and Jesus are invited in and called upon every day. The services are joyous and the prayer is intense. Jesus is adored. The church is a house of prayer. Healing is a focus.

At first, this was all a little beyond my comfort level. There was such joy and adoration expressed, such intense prayer and calls for healing. Part of that did make sense to me, although I had never seen it expressed before. The Eucharist alone is such a fantastic gift, so how could the service not be joyous? But such intense prayer and healing was new. That put God right there in the church. I was much less sure about that.

Since the church is very focused on the gospel, I found my Bible and started reading again. I could not find a single argument in the Bible against anything that I was seeing and experiencing. Actually, everything I read showed that this church was doing it right. Healing and prayer are not beyond what we can ask of God, but they are part of Him. The gospel is not a history book describing only what has passed, but instead it is alive and well. Many feel the Holy Spirit present right there in and among the pews.

As you might expect from this description, St. Paul's got behind Emma 100 percent. A few days after the diagnosis, I understood that my coming to that church was no accident. This was where we should be, where we needed to be, to help us through this. Intense prayer started. Intense healing started, during both the Sunday service and the Wednesday prayer and healing service. There was the laying on of hands and the raising of hands in prayer. The minister, Paul Teske, and his wife, Rivers Teske, prayed for Emma intensely. The youth minister, Scott Tilton, and his wife, Holly Tilton, did so also. Members of the congregation prayed intensely. The entire congregation prayed. I felt we were not alone but that we had a whole community behind us each time we went into the hospital. One Sunday I will never forget is when Emma was in front of the church and the congregation raised their hands in prayer. A guest minister, Michael Koulianos, a young man with a healing and evangelistic ministry, joined Pastor Teske and the congregation in healing prayer for Emma. He prayed that Emma would be healed and would someday meet her grandchildren. A little over one week later, the first CT scan came back with positive results. The following Sunday, I announced the results to the congregation. Everyone jumped to their feet with shouts of joy and praise.

On December 14, Emma's end-of-treatment scan results came in. No more cancer can be detected by any of the scans. It is a miracle. Her oncologist is astounded, and he acknowledges how blessed we are. Of course, we need to go back every three months to check. But for now, Emma has been cured. Prayers were answered, and God cured her cancer. God is alive, and He answers our prayers. We thank Him and all of His servants here among us for their work in righting what is wrong and showing us the power of faith.

What an incredibly awesome God we serve!

THE REASON: THEY ASKED

Occasionally, Jesus healed simply because He was asked to do so. Consider the healing request recorded in Matthew 8:

> *When He had come down from the mountain, great multitudes followed Him. And behold, a leper came and worshiped Him, saying, "Lord, if You are willing, You can make me clean." Then Jesus put out His hand and touched him, saying, "I am willing; be cleansed." Immediately his leprosy was cleansed. And Jesus said to him, "See that you tell no one; but go your way, show yourself to the priest, and offer the gift that Moses commanded, as a testimony to them." (Matthew 8:1-4)*

We need to ask Jesus for healing. The Bible clearly teaches that sometimes we do not receive from God because we simply do not ask Him for what we desire. This issue is addressed in James 4:2: *"Yet you do not have because you do not ask."* At a Wednesday night service in 2005, a woman with a large, white neck brace approached Rivers and me and asked if we would lay hands on her and pray for healing. She told us that she had injured her neck a few years earlier and desired healing. As we began to minister, Rivers received a word of knowledge and spoke directly to the woman's emotional suffering from depression. Rivers prophetically stated that God wanted to set her free. She initially seemed taken aback, but then she proceeded to unveil a history of anxiety and fear that had draped her in depression. We joined together and prayed that the spirits of depression, anxiety, and fear would be lifted off her, and we sent them to the feet of Jesus for judgment. She began to weep, and as she wept, she began to move her neck back and forth—up and down. All of a sudden, she realized her freedom and removed her neck brace. She continued to weep and laugh as she embraced her healing.

How did this healing happen? The physical was tied to demonic oppression. Over the years, oppressive spirits had served as weights on this woman's body. As these spirits were lifted off, what had "compressed" her was gone, and she began to physically "decompress." What was witnessed in the tears and movement was the body decompressing, and with it the skeletal structure became properly aligned. Necks, backs, hips, knees, and ankles are often healed when the spiritual weight of demonic oppression is removed.

Each believer in Jesus Christ has been bought with the blood of Jesus and legally belongs to Him. A true believer cannot be "possessed" by the devil. However, we can create an atmosphere in which Satan can enter into our minds, hearts, or bodies. For instance, anxiety is not of God: *"Anxiety in the heart of man causes depression, but a good word makes it glad"* (Proverbs 12:25). If we become anxious and begin to dwell on our fear, Satan can use this position to create a stronghold of depression in our lives. If the stronghold of depression is removed, then the enemy loses his grip and must flee. The Bible says: *"Therefore submit to God. Resist the devil and he will flee from you"* (James

4:7). He must go, but he will wait for another opportunity: *"Now when the devil had ended every temptation, he departed from Him until an opportune time"* (Luke 4:13). God also gave Cain advice about sin waiting to enter into his life as recorded in Genesis: *"If you do well, will·you not be accepted? And if you do not do well, sin lies at the door. And its desire is for you, but you should rule over it"* (Genesis 4:7). We must be alert and stay washed with Christ's blood.

I traveled to South Africa in June 2005, and I was invited to speak in a Pentecostal church whose congregation consisted of predominantly Caucasian parishioners. Before the service, the pastor's wife told me that she had a bladder problem. She explained that since she was a young girl, she had to urinate every fifteen minutes. She further shared how this had been a major inconvenience in travel, sleeping, and virtually all aspects of her life. I told her that I would pray for her that morning.

The service began with a few minutes of worship before the pastor introduced me. It took me about thirty minutes to share my testimony, after which I stopped to minister to the congregation. I looked straight at the pastor's wife and asked her to come forward. (She later told me that she had not gone out to relieve herself earlier in the service because she did not want to be rude and leave while I was speaking. She had hoped I would call someone else forward, giving her time to leave the sanctuary and void her bladder.) But oblivious to her feelings of discomfort, I called her to the front of the church and anointed her with oil, laid hands on her, and declared her healed in the name of Jesus. She immediately fell to the floor in the Spirit, where she remained for several minutes. When she stood up, her lifetime ailment was completely healed; her bladder was restored to normal functioning. She asked and she received! *"Ask, and it will be given to you; seek, and you will find; knock, and it will be opened to you"* (Matthew 7:7).

Paul Praying for the Sick at Healing Meeting in Prague, Czech Republic (2010).

This woman's spine was severed in an automobile accident. Her friends brought her directly from the hospital and God healed her.

This man was healed of the effects of a stroke he sufferd eight years previously.

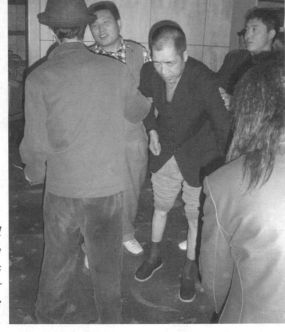

This man had cerebral palsey for 30 years and had never walked before he was healed.

Above: *Rivers in India in 2009.* Below: *Paul and Rivers ministering in Finland (2005).*

Paul preaches during a 2007 crusade in the National Stadium, Kampala, Uganda.

Gregg Healey prays for a crippled boy who was healed in the crusade. Preaching at right is Jackson Senyonga, pastor of Christian Life Ministries, a large church in Kampala, Uganda.

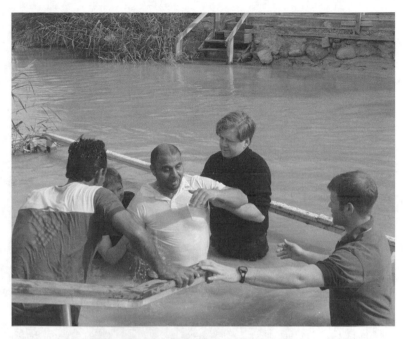

Paul Baptizing Palestinians in the Jordan River near Jericho (2010).

Paul at the Pool of Bethesda in the Arab Quarter of Old Jerusalem (2010).

Norwegian Christian Television broadcast with Paul, his grandson Tyler, and TV Host (2007).

Rivers, Paul, and Pastor Fridrik on Christian Television in Iceland (2008).

How Did Jesus Heal?

I have been asked many times if Jesus had a formula for healing. I believe He did, and the answer to this question is revealed in the Bible. About healing, it teaches that Jesus only did what He heard His Father direct Him to do.

> Then Jesus answered and said to them, "Most assuredly, I say to you, the Son can do nothing of Himself, but what He sees the Father do; for whatever He does, the Son also does in like manner. For the Father loves the Son, and shows Him all things that He Himself does; and He will show Him greater works than these, that you may marvel. For as the Father raises the dead and gives life to them, even so the Son gives life to whom He will." (John 5:19-21)

Spiritually Jesus saw and heard what His Father wanted Him to do, and then He walked it out in obedience. And the results were amazing.

JESUS HEALED IN CROWDS

There are several instances in Scripture when Jesus had entire towns come to Him for healing and deliverance, but no better example is there than the account in Mark 1:

At evening, when the sun had set, they brought to Him all who were sick and those who were demon-possessed. And the whole city was gathered together at the door. Then He healed many who were sick with various diseases, and cast out many demons; and He did not allow the demons to speak, because they knew Him. (Mark 1:32-34)

Rivers and I were invited to speak at a large gathering of believers who met annually in St. Andrews, Scotland. For three days I spoke in a large tent that seated about 3,000 people, and at the end of each session, I prayed for healing. With such a large crowd, it was physically impossible to individually anoint them with oil and lay hands on every person, so I prayed collectively for healing. Group healing prayers, such as took place in Scotland, may seem insincere to an unbeliever, but to people of faith who want a touch from the Lord, it can be a most amazing experience. At the end of the third day, I asked how many attendees had experienced a healing, and several hundred people raised their hands.

We have ministered in numerous large venues where God's power has released healing and deliverance into the masses. When God's presence comes, His glory comes; and when His glory comes, so does His power. The truth is this: When the power of God arrives in a place—large or small—broken things are made whole.

JESUS HEALED INDIVIDUALS

Then Peter opened his mouth and said: "In truth I perceive that God shows no partiality. But in every nation whoever fears Him and works righteousness is accepted by Him." (Acts 10:34-35)

The Bible clearly states that God does not discriminate. The Greek word for *partiality* implies "showing favoritism; exhibiting bias; showing discrimination; treating one better than another." While people make distinctions among other people, God's love and grace are available for all and can be received by everyone. Jesus, the Son of God, healed men, women, young people, rich, poor, Gentiles, and Jews. He did not care where He was or whom He was with; He healed as His Father directed Him.

For you are all sons of God through faith in Christ Jesus. For as many of you as were baptized into Christ have put on Christ. There is neither Jew nor Greek, there is neither slave nor free, there is neither male nor female; for you are all one in Christ Jesus. And if you are Christ's, then you are Abraham's seed, and heirs according to the promise. (Galatians 3:26-29)

A wonderful example of Jesus indiscriminately healing is found in Luke 14:1-4:

Now it happened, as He went into the house of one of the rulers of the Pharisees to eat bread on the Sabbath, that they watched Him closely. And behold, there was a certain man before Him who had dropsy. And Jesus, answering, spoke to the lawyers and Pharisees, saying, "Is it lawful to heal on the Sabbath?" But they kept silent. And He took him and healed him, and let him go.

While visiting friends in Baltimore, Maryland, a businessman called Rivers and me to see if we would pray for his daughter. She was in her mid-thirties and had breast cancer, and the family was fearful that it might metastasize into other parts of her body. We made arrangements to meet her at the place where we were staying. Upon arriving, she seemed nervous and apprehensive, unsure of what we might say or do. I explained how God had healed me and was using us in the healing ministry. Even though she attended a mainline church where the gifts of the Spirit were not emphasized, she seemed to have peace with our offer. We anointed her head with oil and laid our hands on her. We prayed for complete healing and then she left.

About twelve months later, I received an out-of-the-blue phone call from her father. He refreshed my memory about who he was and then reported that his daughter was cancer-free and thanked us for our prayers. I told him to thank Jesus, for He was the healer and we were just the vessels He used to do His work.

Many times we have not seen immediate healing or deliverance results while praying. The absence of immediate healing by no means implies that people are not healed. God alone knows the timing of His plans. Only once in a while, God allows us to see the fruit of His healing hands. We've come to know that whether we see the fruit or not does not mean that God is not at work, but certainly hearing a report of healing, like that one from DC, boosts our hearts to new levels of joy.

JESUS HEALED IMMEDIATELY

There are, of course, accounts of power when Jesus prayed and instant healing occurred. One such well-known healing episode is reported in Luke 13:

> *Now He was teaching in one of the synagogues on the Sabbath. And behold, there was a woman who had a spirit of infirmity eighteen years, and was bent over and could in no way raise herself up. But when Jesus saw her, He called her to Him and said to her, "Woman, you are loosed from your infirmity." And He laid His hands on her, and immediately she was made straight, and glorified God. (Luke 13:10-13)*

After my stroke, the neurologist gave me anti-seizure medication, which I was obliged to take for three months. Even though I had not had a seizure, my doctor felt it was a necessary precaution to prevent any possibility of seizures. One of the major downsides to taking this medication was that I was considered "unfit" to drive. Fortunately, I had several people in my congregation who cheerfully volunteered to drive me where I needed to go. Lars Lindstrom was one such dear saint who drove me about town on a near daily basis.

It was midafternoon on a Wednesday, and Lars and I had just left my doctor's office. We were en route to my office in Westport when we passed a Christian bookstore and I asked him to stop. My motive was to bless Lars by purchasing him a new Bible, yet God had more planned. We walked into the shop, which was narrow and long. At its end was a small counter with a middle-aged woman standing

131

behind it. I asked where the Bible section was, and the shopkeeper pointed to a section against the wall. I perused the selection of Bibles but could not find the particular text I was looking for, so I asked clerk if she carried the NKJV version I wanted. She did not have it in stock, but said she could order it for me. We worked through this order, and I paid her for the Bible.

As we started to leave the store, a thought came to mind and I looked to see if there were any posters for our upcoming Friday's evening healing service. I had invited a friend, Alvin Slaughter, to lead the worship, so I was curious if our promotion efforts had reached this shop. I asked her if she had received any flyers for the special service, and to my surprise, she responded by asking if I was Pastor Teske. I was truly surprised. I told her that I was, and she immediately asked if I would pray for her back. Her symptoms had started twelve months earlier, when she had contracted a bacterial infection in the spinal cord and was treated with routine antibiotics. The infection had cleared up, but she still had severe pain in her back. She often could not even come to work as the pain was so great. It was only a last-minute decision that she came that very day because her daughter—the store manager—had a family commitment elsewhere. She also shared that she had considered closing the store due to her condition, but she needed the revenue. "Might we also pray for my business?" she asked, so Lars and I prayed that God would bless her and that she would have every need met, lacking for nothing.

While Lars and I prayed, the front door opened and a woman came in to browse. While observing the potential customer, I asked her if she would like us to stop or continue praying. She asked us to continue. I reached in my pocket and took out the oil and I anointed her head by reaching over the counter. I then told her to place her hands in mine and I prayed that God would heal her of her back pain. As I began my prayer, she slowly started to fall to her left, and then all at once, she was down on the floor. Out like a light! I looked around at the lone customer to see her reaction and explained that I had just prayed for the shopkeeper. The lady slowly approached the counter. As she did, I told her my name and that I was a Lutheran pastor. "I am Lutheran," she said. That gave me the opening to explain what had happened. She mutely stared at me for a few minutes and left the store with no further interaction. A seed was planted.

After about ten minutes, the woman opened her eyes, and Lars and I helped her to her feet. I asked her how she felt and she replied that she was woozy, but her back felt better. I gave her my card and we left for my office.

My cell phone rang about two hours later. The voice on the other end of the phone was ecstatic. It was the woman from the bookstore. I could hear loud praise music playing in the background. She excitedly said all the back pain was gone and that she was able to run up and down the aisles in her store, praising God for her healing. I asked her if she would come on Friday night to the healing service and give her testimony. She said, "Yes and thank you." I told her to thank Jesus; He is the healer.

Friday night came and the church was packed. I saw her sitting in the front. After welcoming the crowd (I was the "warm up band" that night), I invited her up to share her story. She told the audience every detail about her healing.

She discussed how on that day we prayed she had had the best day of sales in a long while. She also added that she had been praying for God to heal her so she could go on a mission trip to Brazil. Her back condition had made it impossible for her to sit on an airplane for a long international flight, but now, because God had completely healed her back, she was going on her first mission trip. Then, to the surprise of us all, she took out a pair of scissors and her handicapped parking sticker and began to cut it up, throwing the pieces into the air. She shouted, "I don't need it anymore; God healed me!" The audience roared!

Before the worship leader began to play, Alvin proclaimed that this was the real Church: taking the power of God to the marketplace. He then launched into a powerful night of worship.

JESUS HEALED INCREMENTALLY

In Mark 8, Jesus had to pray for a man twice before he was completely healed. This interesting account helps us understand incremental healings.

> *Then He came to Bethsaida; and they brought a blind man to Him, and begged Him to touch him. So He took the blind man by the hand and led him out of the town. And when He had spit on his eyes and put His hands on him, He asked him if he saw anything. And he looked up and said, "I see men like trees, walking." Then He put His hands on his eyes again and made him look up. And he was restored and saw everyone clearly.* (Mark 8:22-25)

Rivers and I were ministering in southern India to a large crowd who had gathered for a four-day crusade in an open field. The host pastor had planted a church in the community and was using the crusade as a vehicle to seed the fellowship. The open field just outside of town was ringed with vertical fluorescent lights fastened to poles. Inside the perimeter of these lights stood two thousand people hungry for the Lord. The speaker platform was separated from the crowd by a rope banister, and at the end of each evening, Rivers and I would walk the rope line to pray for the sick. On our first night, a small child was brought to the front. Her feet were curled up under her body, and we were told she had never walked. We prayed intensely for God to heal her, but nothing seemed to happen.

The second night, we were back on the rope line praying for the infirmed. The mother of the young girl was again present, holding her daughter. We noticed that her legs seemed to have straightened out a bit from the previous night. We prayed again. On the third night, her legs were hanging down, but she still would not put any weight on them. Once again, we prayed for her. By the fourth night, she was standing on both legs, which were able to hold her little body. A miracle had been occurring over time to the glory of God. We never saw her again and did not receive any reports about her, but I am sure that God completed the healing to bear witness to the power of Jesus in that village.

JESUS HEALED PEOPLE ON THE MOVE

In one biblical account of healing, Jesus spoke a healing word and sent the men on their way, telling them that they would be healed as they walked.

Now it happened as He went to Jerusalem that He passed through the midst of Samaria and Galilee. Then as He entered a certain village, there met Him ten men who were lepers, who stood afar off. And they lifted up their voices and said, "Jesus, Master, have mercy on us!" So when He saw them, He said to them, "Go, show yourselves to the priests." And so it was that as they went, they were cleansed. (Luke 17:11-14)

I spoke at a large gathering of charismatic Lutherans in the Midwest. As was my usual practice, after I shared my testimony, I began to pray for the people. One of the first to make it to the platform was the host pastor's secretary, who brought up her mother with a serious knee injury. The younger woman asked me to pray for her mother as she was facing surgery for her knee. I asked the mother if she felt any pain or discomfort, to which she responded, "Yes." As Jesus did in the Luke 17 account, I told her to walk back and forth across the platform and she would be healed as she walked. She obeyed me and began to walk. Indeed, the pain left her and she felt her knee grow stronger. She began to cry tears of joy as she believed God healed her in that moment.

JESUS HEALED BY HIS TOUCH

There are also several places in the Bible where Jesus reached out and touched people; His mere touch brought them healing. One example of this is found in Matthew 20:

Now as they went out of Jericho, a great multitude followed Him. And behold, two blind men sitting by the road, when they heard that Jesus was passing by, cried out, saying, "Have mercy on us, O Lord, Son of David!" Then the multitude warned them that they should be quiet; but they cried out all the more, saying, "Have mercy on us, O Lord, Son of David!" So Jesus stood still and called them, and said, "What do you want Me to do for you?" They said to Him, "Lord, that our eyes may be opened." So Jesus had compassion and touched their eyes. And immediately their eyes received sight, and they followed Him. (Matthew 20:29-34)

In January 2007, Rivers and I took a ministry team from our church to Kampala, Uganda. We were teaching leaders, working with orphans and widows, and conducting healing and deliverance services. One afternoon, a senior leader in the national government came to our room at the hotel for prayer. After a time of sharing, Rivers asked the official if she could pray for him, and as she started, I stood beside the man and placed my hand on the small of his back. I said nothing as I prayed with a hope that the man would be open to receive from God whatever God wanted to do for him.

After Rivers concluded her prayer for him, he turned to me and said that he felt heat radiating from my hand into his back. He bent over several times and started swaying back and forth as if to test his body. He then told us that he had come with a severe back pain that he had not mentioned. In an instant, his back was completely healed by a touch from Jesus on his back.

JESUS HEALED THOSE WHO TOUCHED HIM

I cannot count the times that Rivers and I have walked through dense crowds in India, Africa, and China on our

way to platforms to speak, and we have people reach out to touch us. I have never felt the power of God flow through me when someone touched me, but Rivers has on numerous occasions felt the power of God course through her veins. I believe that God in His mercy and compassion has released healing to some of those who have touched us. We are the Body of Christ, and Jesus declared that His Body would do the same works that He did, as evidenced by Matthew 14:

> *When they had crossed over, they came to the land of Gennesaret. And when the men of that place recognized Him, they sent out into all that surrounding region, brought to Him all who were sick, and begged Him that they might only touch the hem of His garment. And as many as touched it were made perfectly well. (Matthew 14:34-36)*

JESUS HEALED
THROUGH THE SPOKEN WORD

Jesus was the Word made flesh. When He spoke, the power of God was released.

> *Again, departing from the region of Tyre and Sidon, He came through the midst of the region of Decapolis to the Sea of Galilee. Then they brought to Him one who was deaf and had an impediment in his speech, and they begged Him to put His hand on him. And He took him aside from the multitude, and put His fingers in his ears, and He spat and touched his tongue. Then, looking up to heaven, He sighed, and said to him, "Ephphatha," that is, "Be opened." Immediately his ears were opened, and the*

impediment of his tongue was loosed, and he spoke plainly. (Mark 7:31-35)

I have spoken a healing word into a person's circumstance numerous times. Once, a young minister from Florida came to spend a few days with Rivers and me to be mentored. One evening, he called home to speak to his wife and two-year-old son. On that night his son had a high fever, and his wife was concerned. He asked me if I would pray with his wife for his son over the phone. As I prayed, I asked Jesus to rebuke the fever and heal the child. My prayer harkened back to Romans 4:17: *"God, who gives life to the dead and calls those things which do not exist as though they did."* Here we learn that we must speak into that which is not as though it were, and it becomes what we proclaim. For his son, and for every other person we have ever prayed over, we declare health into a sick body as though it was healthy, and it becomes what we declare—healthy! The next morning, he received a good news call: The baby's fever was gone, and he was doing well.

JESUS HEALED THROUGH STRANGE METHODS

Jesus sometimes used strange methods to release healing into people's lives, as testified to in John 9:

When He had said these things, He spat on the ground and made clay with the saliva; and He anointed the eyes of the blind man with the clay. And He said to him, "Go, wash in the pool of Siloam" (which is translated, Sent). So he went and washed, and came back seeing. (John 9:6-7)

I cannot remember being instructed by the Lord to do anything strange like cover a man's eyes with mud and then have him wash it off. I do have some very interesting stories that seem strange and out of the ordinary (as if healing and deliverance are ordinary in the natural world to begin with!).

Rivers and I were ministering in a large church in Cape Town, South Africa, to about two thousand people. I was teaching on healing and deliverance and wanted to demonstrate how God reveals healing is about to occur through a word of knowledge. I explained that sometimes God will give a thought or word to a person about an area of healing that is not their own. A man raised his hand and said he had such a word come to his mind. It was "worms." I asked if anyone had worms and no one responded. Not one person raised their hands to the need of being healed of "worms." We moved on and several others shared a number of issues that needed healing, such as necks, feet, backs, cancers, etc. I then asked people to stand if they had one of the secondary issues mentioned. Many people stood, and we prayed for them.

The session ended, and people began to file out of the auditorium. A few remained behind to ask questions or to request special prayers. Eventually, two men came up to me. One of the men asked me if I could pray for his friend who had worms and explained that his friend had been too embarrassed to announce publicly that he had a parasite infestation. I prayed for him. Afterward, I sought out the man who had identified the word "worms." I wanted him to know that he was accurate with what God had spoken to him, and I wanted to affirm his obedience to be bold for God.

12

The Position of the First-century Church

The first-century Church elevates the Cross of Christ to its primary focal point. The Crucifixion, where the Lamb of God shed His precious blood to atone for the sins of the world, reflects the centrality of the gospel. John 3:16, referred to by some as "the gospel in a nutshell," says: *"For God so loved the world that He gave His only begotten Son, that whoever believes in Him should not perish but have everlasting life"* (John 3:16).

The Bible clearly states that there is no other name under Heaven whereby one can be saved but by the name of Jesus. Apart from the Cross, the world would not have a means to enter into a loving relationship with the heavenly Father. In the seminary, I was taught to kneel at the foot of the Cross weekly to confess sin and receive absolution, or forgiveness. This weekly penitential exercise is repeated over and over again in liturgical churches throughout the world. Only periodically is the Resurrection celebrated, such as at funeral services and, of course, at Easter. Even less proclaimed is the Ascension of Jesus into Heaven forty days after the Resurrection, which fell on Thursday and received little attention. Pentecost Sunday, enveloped in red, came and went without much fanfare. All of these events are confessed in the creeds of the Church, but the primary weekly focus for the Church remained on the Cross.

Now contrast this Church today with the first followers of Jesus. The comparison is striking. The disciples were scattered on the first Good Friday—at the experience of the Cross—except for John and a few women. The morning of the first Resurrection reports the apostles hiding in a room, only to see Jesus when He sought them out, and even then, those who were not present did not believe the multiple reports of a risen Christ. Even after they saw Him in the flesh, they struggled to accept the fact that He had risen and was alive. During the last forty days of Jesus' time on Earth, He taught them great lessons for walking in power. Yet in spite of everything Jesus told them, they still looked for the reestablishment of the kingdom of Israel. As He ascended to Heaven, they stood bewildered. How was Jesus ever to take over the earthly kingdom if He left them? Throughout the final ten days before Pentecost, they were still working on organizational issues and conducting a congregational meeting to elect new leadership. Then, after all this confusion and change, 120 souls gathered in the upper room waiting for the "gift" the Father would send them as Jesus had promised.

The morning of the first Pentecost came with the fire of the Holy Spirit, and the upper room followers of Jesus found new birth in His power. In Mark 16, we find the key for the success of the early Church moving out from Pentecost. The text says:

> *So then, after the Lord had spoken to them, He was received up into heaven, and sat down at the right hand of God. And they went out and*

preached everywhere, the Lord working with them and confirming the word through the accompanying signs. Amen. (Mark 16:19-20)

The first-century Church did not live at the foot of the empty Cross, but rather it was under the throne of Jesus Christ. They did not linger at the empty tomb, nor did they stand peering at the clouds. They stood firmly under the throne of Christ and moved in His power. Because they knew the authority of Jesus and the role they had as true ambassadors of His Kingdom, they went out in power and Jesus "worked with them," confirming the message with signs, wonders, and miracles. This early band of men and women moved not in their own power and strength, but in the power of the name of Jesus.

Seminary taught me that all signs, wonders, and miracles ended in the first century. It was much later that the Lord pointed me toward a different conclusion concerning this teaching. In fact, He did so through traditional study, but also with many personal experiences of signs and wonders and miracles. I first discovered that there was no evidence in Scripture that signs, wonders, and miracles had ceased at the last breath of the last apostle. On the contrary, there were viable reports during the next three hundred years by Church fathers that miracles continued. Second, I realized that we only speak out of our own experience. I was taught by those who had never experienced a healing miracle. My professors were like the blind leading the blind. And I accepted their dogma ... initially.

The Holy Spirit then taught me, in a most personal way, to live under the throne of Jesus—a place where He returned to His rightful place of power in Heaven and on

Earth. The Bible teaches that all things were created for, by, and through Jesus, and He has authority over everything in creation—every demon, disease, marriage, job, person. Everything is under His authority.

> *He is the image of the invisible God, the firstborn over all creation. For by Him all things were created that are in heaven and that are on earth, visible and invisible, whether thrones or dominions or principalities or powers. All things were created through Him and for Him. He is before all things, and in Him all things consist.* (Colossians 1:15-17)

Furthermore, Christ has given His name to the Church to use in power. The Word declares that Jesus defeated the enemy—death, the devil, sin—at the Cross and that by His *"stripes we are healed"* (Isaiah 53:5). I believe the Body of Christ in the twenty-first century is to be no different from the Body of Christ in the first century. The Church needs to return to its rightful position under the throne of Jesus and believe that He will work to confirm His message with signs and wonders. The threefold ministry of Jesus, which includes healing and deliverance, is to be modeled by His Church today. The Church needs to take hold of the throne of Jesus with one hand and lay the other hand on the sick and demon-possessed to release restorative power.

In December 2005, a messianic believer told me about a Lutheran pastor in Scandinavia who was healed of cancer fifteen years earlier and through whom God had launched a mighty healing ministry. My friend also told me that this pastor had relapsed six months earlier, and was diagnosed with fourth-stage lymphoma. God impressed upon me the need to meet this pastor, so I tracked down his ministry on the Internet. The site had a small box with an English translation of the ministry and the pastor's testimony. In January 2006, I emailed him, sharing my testimony and offering to fly to pray for his healing. It only took a few days for me to receive a return email asking me to come. I told my elders about the circumstance and how Rivers and I felt led to go to Scandinavia to pray for him. They agreed.

On the flight over to Scandinavia, I asked the Lord to give me a *rhema* word from the Scriptures for confirmation regarding our odyssey to the pastor with cancer. God impressed a passage from Romans on my heart: *"As it is written, 'I have made you a father of many nations' in the presence of Him whom he believed—God, who gives life to the dead and calls those things which do not exist as though they did ..."* (Romans 4:17). I knew immediately that this was the *rhema* word for our journey.

We arrived in Scandinavia on a cold Monday evening and were picked up by a local church pastor. The next day, he drove us to the town of the minister; we were to meet him at a local sports hall where he had been holding healing meetings for several years. They met in the sports hall, as the State Lutheran Church had removed him from his parish duties because the ecclesiastical hierarchy did not believe in healing or deliverance. The officials had not removed his ordination credentials, but they did not want him serving a local church parish. We were ushered into a small office and waited.

The Lutheran pastor came in with a young aide and sat down. He told us that he had just come from the hospital to meet us, and that he would return after our visit. His ashen face made him look twenty years older than his real age, and he had an IV line attached to his arm. He told us he was extremely exhausted and apologized for sitting while we spoke. We shared our histories and exchanged the curiosities of how God had used us both. (Rivers later confided to me that "he looked like death" to her.) Since God had commissioned my journey to him, I felt compelled to give him the passage from Romans. As I quoted the verse to him, his aide almost fell out of his chair. With great astonishment, the pastor shared that he, his wife, and his aide had been praying for a word from God of confirmation on the previous Saturday. The Lord had given them the Romans passage also. Here was a clear and glorious sign.

We continued to talk for a short while. I felt a powerful leading by the Holy Spirit to speak, and from my mouth came these words: "This might sound strange, but you have no cancer in your body." I asked if we could celebrate Communion as a reminder that Jesus is both a healer and a redeemer. The pastor responded with joy. Since he had been removed from his church ten years earlier, he had not been able to celebrate Communion, as directed by his bishop. His aide brought in the Communion elements, and we broke bread in his office. I remember consecrating the bread and fruit of the vine saying, "This is the body of Jesus broken for your healing, that by His stripes you would be healed. This is the blood of Jesus shed, that all your sins would be washed away." As we shared the sacrament, I quoted Psalm 103:3: *"Who forgives all your iniquities, who heals all your diseases."*

Immediately I noticed the pastor's skin flush with color. He smiled as he spoke and then offered Rivers and me a tour of the sport facilities. He walked throughout the place with no apparent effort or sign of fatigue. Forty minutes later, his son arrived and told him he would need to return him to the hospital. We said our farewells, and Rivers and I got into our automobile. Rivers exclaimed, "I cannot believe you were so bold! This will be a mighty miracle if he is healed." We were taken back to the airport, where we caught a flight back to New York. I knew God had healed the pastor.

One week later I received an email from the pastor in Scandinavia. His email started with an apology and an explanation. He reported that he had been receiving chemotherapy since December 2004, and a week before Rivers and I arrived, the physicians had decided to test him to see if the therapy was having an effect on the tumors. If not, he, his wife, and his oncologist had decided to end the exhaustive cancer protocol immediately. There would be no other protocol offered. His email continued that the Friday before we met, the report had come back that he had no cancer in his body. On Saturday, he, his wife, and his aide had asked the Lord for a confirmation, and God had given them Romans 4: 17. So with great surprise and hope, he could not believe that I gave him the very same passage three days later, and that I went on to say he had no cancer in his body. He thought, *How could Teske know that? Only my wife, aide, physician, and I know this.* He said that he was so confused and overwhelmed by our conversation that he did not know what to say. But he believed.

Four years later, this Scandinavian pastor's ministry is still going strong. He has been removed from the roster of the state church, but I do not believe it matters a great deal to him, as he is in full-throttle doing kingdom work. Malachi 3:6 says, *"For I am the Lord, I do not change ..."*

Jesus is the same yesterday, today, and forever. We are the Body of Christ, and our mission is to continue to do what the head of the Body, Jesus Christ, called us to do—teach, preach, and heal.

13

Raising the Bar of Faith

People frequently ask me, "What if you pray for someone and they are not healed?" My response takes them to unchartered waters. I usually say how every Sunday I preach the Gospel of Jesus Christ crucified and risen, but not everyone is saved. I do not stop preaching just because I do not have a 100 percent acceptance of Jesus Christ as one's Lord and Savior. The same is true when I anoint the sick with oil for healing and deliverance. Because everyone is not healed or delivered does not mean that I will quit walking in obedience to the Word of God found in James 5.

> *Is anyone among you suffering? Let him pray. Is anyone cheerful? Let him sing psalms. Is anyone among you sick? Let him call for the elders of the church, and let them pray over him, anointing him with oil in the name of the Lord. And the prayer of faith will save the sick person, and the Lord will raise him up. And if he has committed sins, he will be forgiven.* (James 5:13-15)

God has impressed on my heart and mind that my role is do my part and let God do His part. An excellent example is found in the Book of Exodus.

After a glorious exodus from Egypt, Moses and the Israelites faced their first major obstacle—the Red Sea.

Mountains on either side were preventing them from escaping left or right. Pharaoh was closing in from behind with an army of chariots equipped with the latest technology of armament. The people, having given up hope of survival, began to complain and cry out to Moses, demanding his immediate solution to their predicament. Moses in turn cried out to God. God's response is worth noting. He basically told Moses, "Why are you crying out to me?" Moses must have thought, *What else can I do?* God's answer surpassed human understanding—even wise Moses' understanding. In essence, God said to Moses, "What do you have in your hand?" Moses looked at the staff he had been carrying before Pharaoh. "A staff," he replied. God then told Moses to do his part and raise the staff before the waters of the Red Sea. Why? Moses had to do his part so God could do His part, which was to miraculously part the waters so that His people could escape to freedom. We all know the conclusion of the story. The people crossed over, and as Pharaoh's army pursued, they were drowned in the sea.

In the healing and deliverance ministry, God calls us to do our part—to anoint the sick with oil, to lay hands on them, and to pray for healing and deliverance. Once we comply with our role, then God is released to heal and deliver.

The game of baseball is another excellent illustration for roles. Picture yourself as the baseball pitcher and God as the batter. You must throw the pitch so God can hit the ball. You say, "What if you do not hit my pitch?" God responds, "You throw the ball, and I will hit it." You hesitate and say, "Okay, but what if you do not hit it?" God again says,

"Throw the ball; I will hit it." You again challenge God and say, "I hear you, but ..." God shouts, "You can throw the ball in the dirt! You can throw it over the backstop! You can throw it out in left field! It does not matter. I will hit it; but I cannot hit it if you do not throw the pitch!"

This analogy illustrates the difficulty we have with trusting God to do His part. All He asks us to do is our part: to be obedient and to lay hands on the sick and anoint them with oil. Then God is released to heal and deliver. As God provided Moses with the staff in his hand, so He has provided us with the oil in our hands. We simply have to exercise our faith and raise the staff. The reason we struggle with this request is because we do not trust God to honor His part of the agreement. We do not trust, and therefore, we do not experience.

Every Sunday, Christians around the world declare their faith in the resurrection from the dead. This bold statement of faith—that someday, a pile of dust will rise and live again for all eternity—no one can prove in the natural. But we declare it so. Yet today's Church struggles to believe that the same God who will raise us from the dead can heal the incurable or make the lame walk, make the blind see, make the deaf hear, or kick out demons that torment His people. The questions plaguing the Church are these: Can we really trust God? Does He know what He is doing? Is He really good? If the answer is no to any of these questions, then we have a real problem.

The Bible teaches us in Titus 1:2 that God cannot lie: *"... God, who cannot lie ..."* John 14:6 declares that Jesus Christ is the truth: *"Jesus said to him, 'I am the way, the truth, and the life. No one comes to the Father except through Me.'"*

The Scriptures teach us the Holy Spirit is the agent of truth: *"However, when He, the Spirit of truth, has come, He will guide you into all truth ..."* (John 16:13). If these are statements from the Bible that we claim to be true, then we must learn to embrace the Word and apply its truth to stand on it in every ministry opportunity, including healing and deliverance.

In 2 Corinthians 5:7, we are challenged: *"For we walk by faith, not by sight."* In Hebrews 11:1, we are given an understanding about our faith: *"Now faith is the substance of things hoped for, the evidence of things not seen."* Faith is substance, not wishful thinking. The substance of our faith must be seen in the spiritual realm and create an expectation that what we are praying for will become a reality. Too often it is our experience that establishes our level of faith. Experience pulls faith down to the level of what we experience in the natural. We should not walk by experience (fact), but by faith, believing in the outcome we have not yet experienced. We should allow our faith to rise to a level above our natural experience and let the experience catch up with our faith.

When a person is diagnosed with cancer, our experience begins to frame our response. Hopelessness and acceptance of the world's statistics concerning outcomes, including treatments and reliance on physicians, take root in our minds. People very seldom turn first to God with expectancy for healing. Normally, the diagnosis is followed by a prognosis from a medical authority, which then becomes the accepted norm. Let me give you an illustration. On a

Saturday morning in June 2005, I sat on my porch praying and meditating for a three-week trip to South Africa and Zimbabwe, which would begin the next day. The phone rang. One of my parishioners, Ellen Knapp, reported that her young niece who lived in a Midwestern city had a two-year-old son with leukemia. The boy had been receiving treatment, but after three rounds of chemotherapy, the leukemia had returned with vengeance. The prognosis was to abandon the protocol and all the hope that went with it. Distraught, Ellen's niece left her family at the hospital. Ellen asked me to call the upset mother and pray with her, in hopes that it might quiet her heart. I agreed.

I immediately called the young mother and had a lengthy telephone conversation. She belonged to a traditional, mainline church and expressed a nominal relationship with the Lord. I asked her permission to pray for her son, her marriage, and her family. It was time for me to do my part. We began to pray and during the prayer, God gave me an unction that I spoke into her life. I told her that her son would not have leukemia and the physicians would be confounded. It was a short statement, but it was straight from the revelation of God. After hanging up, I called Ellen—my church member—to give her an update. The next day, I left for South Africa.

The following Sunday, I called my wife to give a progress report on my trip. She told me that she had good news concerning the baby with leukemia. Ellen reported that the leukemia cell count had fallen overnight to half of what it had been on Saturday. By two days later, the count had dropped another 50 percent. By Wednesday, less than a week after our believing prayer, there were no leukemia cells in the child's blood. The pediatric oncologist had no explanation. The family was ecstatic.

About two months later, Ellen reported to me that the family was frustrated with the pediatric oncologist who had "misdiagnosed" the child disease. They were trying to explain the miracle of God in human terms. Ellen and I flew to the Midwestern city to speak and pray with the entire family. I told them that the doctor had not misdiagnosed the leukemia but that God had answered the prayer for healing. Instead of focusing on the physician, I exhorted them to give thanks to God for the miracle that had been requested. I was asking them to abandon human understanding and to "see" with faith the healing that God caused in their circumstance. Four years later, the child continues to be disease-free.

The substance of my faith for the child consisted of no leukemia. Not *less* illness. What I declared as I heard God speak to my heart became the reality we hoped for. I raised the bar of faith above the natural expectations for the child, and the experience caught up with the faith statement—no leukemia. The Church must move from hopefulness to expectancy. I do not hope to rise from the dead; I expect to rise from the dead. We must become a people of expectancy in all areas of our faith walk with Jesus.

14

The Faith Issue

The Bible reports that Jesus healed people with weak faith, strong faith, and normal faith. He healed people because of other people's faith. He healed spontaneously, intermittently, and as people were on the move. The one consistent factor was that His faith never wavered. We must learn from Jesus.

> *Is anyone among you sick? Let him call for the elders of the church, and let them pray over him, anointing him with oil in the name of the Lord. And the prayer of faith will save the sick, and the Lord will raise him up. And if he has committed sins, he will be forgiven. Confess your trespasses to one another, and pray for one another, that you may be healed. The effective, fervent prayer of a righteous man avails much.* (James 5:14-16)

Not so long ago, I visited a city in an isolated mountain region of China. The primary religious groups inhabiting that area were Muslims and Buddhists. An American businessman who works in the region arranged for me to meet with local Christian leaders to teach them about healing and deliverance. On the first day the businessman drove me to a hotel off-limits to Western people. (The government controls hotel usage and limits the number of approved hotels for Western travelers.) The hotel was located in a predominantly Muslim neighborhood, so we entered the rear door of the building. Sporadic fireworks for the last day of Ramadan broke the silence of the neighborhood. We climbed the narrow stairs and entered a room forty feet wide and eighty feet long packed with about five hundred people. The host pastor came over and introduced himself to me and said through a translator that these people had come for healing. (Everything I said during the meeting needed a translator.) I asked about first teaching the leaders, but he responded that we would heal today and teach tomorrow.

Okay. With five hundred people in the audience, it would require a whole lot of healing time (six hours to be exact!). The room was filled, overflowing, with expectancy. I walked up onto a small platform in the front and asked how many people in the audience believed in Jesus as their Lord and Savior. Fifty hands rose. I then asked my translator to find ten believers and bring them to the small stage. I explained to the elect group of ten that they were to become my healing team. I told them that as the people came forward for healing prayer, I would anoint each person with oil. Afterward, I would send them to one of the team members, who would pray for the specific healing need. I then anointed each of their hands and prayed that God would give them an impartation to release the healing flow of His power.

I then turned toward the audience and explained how we were going to proceed. As I was speaking, a man came through the side door carrying a young man draped over his shoulders like a backpack. Initially I thought the man carried a corpse, but then the body's head moved and I thought, *Thank you, Jesus! He is alive!* I told the crowd that I would anoint everyone with oil for healing and asked the host pastor to serve as head usher, to make sure that the people would come forward in an orderly way. Finally, I reassured the people not to worry, that we would pray for everyone.

I gave a brief gospel presentation followed by an invitation to join me in a commitment prayer. The translator then asked the people to come forward. The man carrying the young man on his back bullied his way through the crowd and stepped onto the platform first. He said his thirty-year-old son suffered from cerebral palsy and had remained bedridden his entire life. According to his testimony, the boy had never walked and as a result, his son's legs had atrophied; they were now the size of a soft drink bottle. He also wore a large makeshift diaper. The father fixed his eyes on me with a mixture of hope and hopelessness. The deafening silence of the room accompanied the testimony, and every eye became fixed on me. The moment of truth had arrived.

God, I spoke silently in my thoughts, *you have got to heal this man. Everyone is watching. There is no turning back. Please heal this man.* I felt like Moses standing in front of the Red Sea. I knew what I had to do. I anointed the man with oil and asked him to give me his hands. I then boldly declared, "In the name of Jesus Christ, walk!" The father stepped aside, and the boy stood wobbling before me. I emphatically said, "In the name of Jesus, walk! Spirit of palsy, I command you to leave now in the name of Jesus." The young man took a step; then another. He slowly walked across the platform, and then turned and slowly walked back to his father. I turned to the astonished crowd and asked who wanted to receive Jesus, who healed this man, as their Lord and Savior. Every hand shot up! For the next six hours I anointed the sick with oil and many healings and deliverances occurred.

The next day, I returned to teach leaders; however, God had other plans. More than a thousand people gathered at the hotel for healing. Just like what happened to the early Acts Church, people lined the halls of the hotel waiting for healing. Friends of a young woman who had her spinal cord severed in an auto accident checked her out of the hospital and brought her to the meeting. As they carried her to the platform, I saw both her feet dragging the floor. She walked out of the meeting praising the Jesus who had healed her. God touched many that day, and the people glorified His name.

The level of faith in those meetings ranged between strong to nonexistent. I knew that my faith had to be at the highest level possible. That was my part. No man can heal another man; Jesus is the healer. My humble role consisted of anointing the sick with oil, laying hands on them, and praying in faith for God to heal. God's part was to be God.

God is no respecter of persons. The same God healing in Asia also heals in other parts of the world, including the United States. Sometimes I see immediate healing, and other times, I have to wait and see. It just takes more faith to wait.

Even today, Jesus can choose to heal a person in stages, like He did for the blind man in Mark 8. I was attending a Presbyterian church in Connecticut on a Sunday evening to hear a guest speaker. At the end of the service, a woman by the name of Paige Stetson came to me and asked me if I was Pastor Teske. When I said that I was, she asked me if I could pray for her eye. She told me that nearly four weeks earlier, while she was walking down the street, all of a sudden, her right eye went dark. She went to the emergency room to have her eye examined and was told that an artery in the back of her eye had ruptured with likely detachment of her retina. After further examination by several ophthalmologists, she was closely monitored for three weeks to see if there would be any improvement. After three weeks, the doctor said they would have to perform a surgical procedure called a vitrectomy and repair the damage. Her surgery was scheduled for that Friday.

I asked her to close her eyes so I could anoint them with oil. I then told her to repeat after me, "Jesus, by your stripes I am healed; I receive my healing; I am thanking you in advance for healing me." I asked her to open her eye and see if there was any improvement. She said, "I would like to say yes, but I still cannot see."

I said, "Well, Jesus prayed for a man twice before he could see; let me pray with you again."

We repeated the same prayer, and again, I asked her if there was any improvement. She replied, "No, but I believe I am healed." I told her that her eye was going to be healed, and she would not need surgery on Friday. She left truly believing that God had heard her prayer and that she would be healed. She walked away in great faith.

She called me on Tuesday, two days later, and told me that she had gone in to see her physician and that he cancelled the surgery because she had 20/20 vision in her

right eye, with no detachment. She told him about the healing prayer she had received and that she believed Jesus had healed her eye. Her doctor did not understand how the eye had been corrected by prayer, but he was happy for her that she indeed could see again.

The beauty of this healing story is that within a week, good reports came back. Other times, God will allow a significant period of time to pass before the fruit of healing is seen. Talk about a faith-building opportunity! Rivers and I were invited to speak on healing and deliverance to a large gathering in Scotland where we had ministered the prior summer. A woman came up to me and asked if I remembered praying for her daughter the previous year. She pointed to her little five-year-old, who was running around with other children. I told her that we had ministered and prayed for many people and I just could not remember them. She said, "Last year, my daughter had braces on both her legs and used a little pink walker." As soon as she said "pink walker," I immediately remembered the little girl and her mother.

The mother reminded me that Rivers and I had laid hands on her daughter, anointed her with oil, and prayed for healing. She told me that over the next few days, she began to notice that her daughter's legs were growing stronger and stronger; and within a few weeks, the braces came off and she was completely restored. The mother said with tears in her eyes, "You told me that she would be healed and walk again, and just look at her run and play." The mother then proceeded to thank me. "Don't thank me; thank Jesus, for He is the healer. Jesus should receive all the honor and glory for restoring your daughter," I told her. Jesus loves the little children and people of faith.

Imparting the Gift of Healing

God has impressed on my heart that in addition to praying for healing and deliverance, Rivers and I should teach on the subject of healing and deliverance; demonstrate the power of God, who works with us to confirm the Word with miracles; and pray for an impartation of healing and deliverance to be given to those who desire to honor God with this gifting. What we received from God through Pastor Benny Hinn, we impart to others with four attitudes of the heart to consider: patience, obedience, boldness, and humility.

Patience is an absolute requirement for the healing and deliverance ministry. Jesus' healing and deliverance outreach witnessed the full gambit of responses—instant, incremental, delayed, distant, and, in the case of Nazareth, none. He simply did what He heard His Father tell Him to do and waited. Rivers and I have experienced the same results. We anoint the sick with oil, lay hands on them for healing, and declare the truth of God's Word. Then we wait.

Obedience is another key to success for any level of ministry. When God speaks, we obey. Regardless of how the situation seems in the natural world, we know that in the spiritual realm, the reality is different. God calls us to walk in obedience without condition. When God directs, we must obey. Partial obedience and delayed obedience is no different from disobedience.

In addition to obedience, the healing and deliverance ministry allows no room for timidity. A spirit of boldness is required. Our broken world is riddled with disease and infested with demons that, at times, appear to be overwhelming. The normal experiences of life will weigh heavily against the odds of supernatural healing or deliverance when our minds quickly assess the situation and feel highly threatened by the Goliaths standing in front of us. At these times we must remember that *"He who is in* [us] *is greater than he who is in the world"* (1 John 4:4). With my God all things are possible. God did not give me a spirit of timidity, but a spirit of boldness. The command of God is, "Do not hold back! Be bold! Be courageous! Do not look left or right! Do not hold back!"

The greatest leader in the Old Testament was Moses. The Bible also teaches that there was no one more humble than Moses: *"Now the man Moses was very humble, more than all men who were on the face of the earth"* (Numbers 12:3). Moses derived his strength and power from God and not from himself, and he gave God the glory and honor and praise for every accomplishment. He took no credit for himself. The Bible teaches that God loves humility and despises pride (see 1 Peter 5:5 and Proverbs 3:34). I know that I can heal no person. In the world, demons see my natural power and authority as non-threatening to them. God alone is the healer and deliverer, and He deserves all the praise, honor, glory, thanks, and recognition. My prayer is that people will not even remember my name or what I look like after they are healed, but that they will remember the name of Jesus and His healing eyes.

Those who learn to walk in these four attributes—patience, obedience, boldness, and humility—will be blessed to be a blessing to others. Let me share three healing stories of those who received such an impartation for healing and deliverance.

One of my healing team members, Lars Lindstrom, accompanied Rivers and me to Iceland for a series of healing meetings and training sessions. Iceland is approximately the size of Ohio, with a population of 300,000 people, three-fourths of the Icelanders living in the country's southwest corner in the capital city of Reykjavík. The remaining 75,000 people are spread around the perimeter of the island's coast. The first day we arrived, the host pastor took us to the local Christian radio station for a live interview, where I shared my testimony and then gave an overview of what we would be teaching concerning healing and deliverance.

The host pastor told me about a sick child who lived on the opposite side of Iceland and asked me if I would be willing to fly over to the small seaside village and pray for the child. I agreed, and arrangements were made for me to go the next day. He and Lars took me to the airport, where I caught my flight, but before it had even left the terminal, the minister received a call from the radio station. Apparently, a woman had called in and requested that Pastor Teske go to the hospital and pray for her nineteen-year-old grandson, who had experienced a cerebral hemorrhage and was in a coma. She said the doctors predicted that he would only live a few more days. Since I was already en route to the other side of the island, the pastor asked Lars if he would be willing to go and pray for the young man. Lars obediently agreed.

When Lars arrived at the hospital, he was taken to the intensive care unit. As he entered the boy's cubicle, he reported that the boy was comatose with about ten tubes coming out of his body and attached to a respirator. The life-support system was keeping him alive. Lars knew he had only a limited amount of time to be in the room, so he began to pray and then boldly declared, "In the name of Jesus Christ, you are healed." He left the ICU, and we heard nothing more about the young man the entire time we remained in the country.

It was only after we had returned from Iceland that the host pastor sent an email to us stating that the young man had come out of his coma and all his organs and faculties were intact. In fact, he had been released from the hospital four days after Lars had prayed for him. The local Christian radio station had broadcast the good news of God's healing power to the nation. Lars' heart desire was for God to use him in a healing ministry. Just prior to departing for Iceland, he had asked Rivers and me to pray that he would receive an impartation for healing and deliverance. Immediately following this request and impartation, God used Lars and granted his desire.

Lars accompanied Rivers and me and several other team members to Uganda, Africa, for healing meetings, teaching seminars, and orphanage work in January 2007. The host pastor, Jackson Senyonga, had arranged for me to speak to about twenty thousand people in Kampala at the Mandela

National Stadium. The team arrived at the stadium on a hot Sunday morning, and while Rivers and I were taken to a waiting room, the rest of the team spread out to pray and survey the crowds.

One team member, Janet, saw a small boy sitting by a ground-level entrance to the stadium. She went over to investigate and found that he was an eleven-year-old orphan who was severely crippled in his legs and arms. He also was deaf and dumb. Because he could not walk, the woman who brought him had left him by the gate in the shade while she attended the crusade meeting. Janet found Lars and asked him for advice about the boy. Lars told her to anoint the boy with oil and start praying for him. About twenty minutes later, Lars reported that he turned to see the boy standing next to him. He then joined with Janet in prayer and the boy started to walk.

As the crusade began, Rivers and I joined several other pastors in the center of the stadium. We were facing the large crowd seated in the bleachers. An African dance team performed on the stadium track area accompanied by African drums. We noticed a small boy in dingy street clothes dancing and jumping with the costumed dancers. As the host pastor called ushers to have the boy removed to the stands, Lars came out to the podium and told me about the boy's healing. I immediately halted the boy's ejection and had Lars tell the host pastor about the boy. The pastor put his arm around the young man and announced to the crowd that the crippled boy had been healed and had even regained his hearing and speech. The Holy Spirit in Janet and Lars released the miraculous power of God that brought the crowd to their feet, shouting and praising God.

Many other miracles happened that hot, steamy Sunday morning in equatorial East Africa.

The Bible teaches that often *"you do not have because you do not ask"* (James 4:2). Shortly after my own healing, a man of great faith, Preben, came to me and requested an impartation for healing. I prayed that God would honor his heart and give him the gift for healing and deliverance. Preben walked out in faith and began a weekly healing meeting in a local nursing home. It was a humble beginning. Not many people came initially, but God began to use him in a powerful way.

A man came to Preben's meeting one night and received a lifesaving touch from God. The man had struggled with addition to drugs and alcohol for more than twenty years. Though he successfully masked his addictions for many years and had risen to the top of his field in business, the drugs and alcohol eventually took its toll on him. He lost his job, family, and marriage. He also contracted hepatitis C, and his health declined rapidly. His prognosis was death. Little did he know what God had in store for him that evening.

The man went forward to Preben for healing prayer. He was not expectant; he did it only to placate his young son's request to find help. As Preben prayed for him, the addict felt an incredibly bright light engulf him and heat flow through his entire body. God cleansed and restored him instantly. All his cravings for drugs and alcohol were instantaneously gone, and he gave his life to Christ that evening. In addition to his deliverance from his addictions, he was completely cured of hepatitis C. The doctors have tested him several times since and have found absolutely no residue of the virus in his blood—a most creative miracle! Four years later, God has restored virtually everything he had previously lost.

It is important to remember that the Holy Spirit in the believer is the same Spirit that raised Jesus from the dead. The Bible teaches that believers will lay hands on the sick for healing and cast out demons. What Rivers and I received we freely give away to those who will walk in the ministry of healing and deliverance with an attitude of patience, obedience, boldness, and humility. God will ignite the gift in those who seek to serve Him.

16

How to Keep a Healing

In the military, we develop an attack strategy to take a fortress on the top of a mountain. However, we need to develop an entirely different strategy to keep and maintain that stronghold. Healing is no different. One strategy is implemented to receive healing and deliverance; another is needed to maintain that healing or deliverance status.

John 5 records Jesus' visit to the Bethesda pool in Jerusalem, where He found a man who had been suffering from an infirmity for thirty-eight years. Jesus asked him if he wanted to be made well. The man responded by saying, "Sir, I have no one to put me in the pool when the water is stirred up; but while I am coming, another steps down before me." Jesus said to him, "Rise, take your bed and walk." Immediately the man stood up, rolled up his mat, and walked away. Later, Jesus found the man in the Temple and said something of profound importance: "See, you have been made well. Sin no more, lest a worse thing come upon you." The man received a full restoration of his body from Jesus; then Jesus encouraged him to go and maintain his healing by sinning no more.

When we receive a healing or deliverance, it is a gift from God, and we need to take necessary steps to keep

our healthy status. The first step is revealed by God in Ephesians:

> *Finally, my brethren, be strong in the Lord and in the power of His might. Put on the whole armor of God, that you may be able to stand against the wiles of the devil. For we do not wrestle against flesh and blood, but against principalities, against powers, against the rulers of the darkness of this age, against spiritual hosts of wickedness in the heavenly places. Therefore take up the whole armor of God, that you may be able to withstand in the evil day, and having done all, to stand. Stand therefore, having girded your waist with truth, having put on the breastplate of righteousness, and having shod your feet with the preparation of the gospel of peace; above all, taking the shield of faith with which you will be able to quench all the fiery darts of the wicked one. And take the helmet of salvation, and the sword of the Spirit, which is the word of God; praying always with all prayer and supplication in the Spirit, being watchful to this end with all perseverance and supplication for all the saints.* (Ephesians 6:10-18)

We are in a spiritual battle against the spiritual enemies of God. By our own strength and power, we will certainly fail, but equipped by God, we can succeed. God provides several pieces of armor for our protection. The belt of truth protects against the false accusations and lies of the enemy. Specifically, the devil tries to convince us that God has not restored us or that He cannot heal or deliver us. But the Bible teaches otherwise; it promises that the truth will set us free.

It is the breastplate of righteousness that protects our hearts. God loves and accepts us unconditionally through Jesus. He will never abandon or reject us. God knows the heart is vulnerable; therefore, He provides our chest with a protective covering. On our feet God places the shoes of the gospel so we can stand on the rock of salvation and not waver under the assault of the enemy. This solid foundation is unshakable because of the supernatural peace of God that guards our hearts and minds in Christ Jesus. (See Philippians 4:7.)

God also gives us a large shield of faith, which protects us from the fiery darts of the enemy. No matter what the devil throws at us—doubt, despair, fear, shame, guilt, anxiety, worry, death—nothing will penetrate the protective shield that God provides. The helmet of salvation protects our minds—our greatest gift. The ability of the human mind to rationalize and think conceptually separates the human species from every other; yet, too often, the mind is our worst enemy. Why? Because our thoughts can lead us astray. God offers to transform our minds by the power of His Spirit so we can see the things of God by faith and not by sight. God offers powerful protection for our minds.

Lastly, God places in our hands the sword of the Spirit. The Spirit of God is the power that raised Jesus from the dead, and it's the Spirit that gives us new life in Jesus. The Bible refers to us as the temple of the Holy Spirit, out of which He releases kingdom power. Psalm 149:6 says: *"Let the high praises of God be in their mouth, and a two-edged sword in their hand."* The implication here is that the praise that comes out of our mouths is a weapon against the enemy.

We are not left defenseless; we have a mighty weapon to wield—the sword of the Spirit.

One reason God heals is to enable us to wear the armor of God. In the military, wounded soldiers go to the hospital to recover from their wounds. When they are fit for duty, they return to the front line for battle. If a soldier does not recover from his wounds, he goes home. God cannot put His armor on us until we are fit for duty. Our brokenness of heart, mind, body, and relationships needs to be made spiritually whole and healthy before we can wear the battle gear. God does not heal us to go back to our old lifestyles of worldliness; He heals us for the spiritual calling on our lives to serve Him.

Putting on the whole armor of God is one way to maintain the gifts of healing and deliverance, but there are additional steps we can take.

The second step demands that every day, we give God the glory and honor and praise and thanksgiving for the healing or deliverance. Do not give credit to any man—no man can heal another man. Jesus is the healer and deserves all the glory. God can use the medical field—physicians and pharmacology—for healing, but God is the true source for all healing.

Sometimes God uses medicinal means to release healing. In Isaiah 38, Isaiah was told by God to inform King Hezekiah that he was going to die. Hezekiah wept and pleaded with God to heal him. God heard the prayers of the dying king and sent the prophet back to report that God would extend the monarch's life by fifteen years. Isaiah was not told to lay hands on Hezekiah and pray for an instantaneous miracle of healing; instead, he was told to utilize the medical technology of his time: figs. *"Now Isaiah had said, 'Let them take a lump of figs, and apply it as a poultice on the boil, and he shall recover'"* (Isaiah 38:21). If God uses current medical technology to heal, give Him the praise and thanksgiving for the gifts of physicians and medical intervention.

One month after I received my healing in 2004, I had a kidney stone that lodged in my urethra, the small tube that connects the kidney to the bladder. I lay doubled up in severe pain in the emergency area of a local hospital for twenty-three hours. The nurses gave me several injections of morphine, attempting to numb the pain, but to no avail. I cried out to God saying, "You cured me of a debilitating stroke in an instant; why can't you take this pain away?" After several hours, God spoke to me and said, *This pain is not for you.* His response confused me. I thought, *Not for me? That does not make any sense.* As I pondered His words, I had an epiphany. During my entire stroke and through my healing, I had experienced absolutely no pain. God miraculously spared me of physical suffering. I believe God allowed me to experience the harsh pain of the kidney stone to understand the pain and suffering of the people who come to me for healing and deliverance prayer. Two days later, my urologist retrieved the stone and sent me on my way. Even though God used current medical technology for my healing, I still gave Him all the credit. I understood the lesson.

A third step to maintain healing is to stay in the Scriptures with prayer and praise. The Word is truth and will reinforce faith. The Bible teaches in Romans that *"faith comes by hearing, and hearing by the word of God"* (Romans 10:17). In dialogue with God (prayer), God confirms in our hearts and minds the great miracles that He has worked in us. In continuous praise and thanksgiving, we keep a proper perspective about the true source for our healing and deliverance.

A fourth and vital step in maintaining a healing miracle is to associate with people who share in faith and will confirm the healing. If we surround ourselves with negative people who doubt God and His power to heal, we will face an uphill battle trying to convince them that there has been a healing miracle. Instead, find people who will celebrate and accept the healing gift with you.

A final way to reinforce healing is to give your testimony. And often. Every day I try to share my healing story with someone. Why? This vocalization builds my faith as well as theirs. When we hear about the miracles of God, how He is alive and active today, the level of our faith rises. The Bible teaches in Hebrews that *"faith is the substance of things hoped for"* (11:1). Malachi 3:6 teaches, *"For I am the LORD, I do not change."* Jesus is the same yesterday, today, and forever. Our testimony confirms a biblical truth—Jesus heals.

17

Regaining the Birthright

How do we restore the healing priority of Jesus' ministry to the Body of Christ? Here is a start. It is not a definitive list, but an attempt to identify what to pray for when seeking a ministry of healing and deliverance.

1. Remember that Jesus has ascended to the throne of Heaven. All authority has been given to Him. He is the Creator, and all of creation is under His control. Colossians 1:15-16 says:

He is the image of the invisible God, the firstborn over all creation. For by Him all things were created that are in heaven and that are on earth, visible and invisible, whether thrones or dominions or principalities or powers. All things were created through Him and for Him.

2. Believe God when He speaks through His Word. In Psalm 103:3, God declares through the psalmist that He forgives all our sins and He heals all our diseases. Jesus speaks only the truth, so when He speaks, He cannot renege on His Word. In John 14:12, Jesus declares that we will do greater works than He. Again, this verse is more than an invitation to move in power; it is an admonition to the Church to be an extension of His ministry.

3. Realize that you are a temple of the Holy Spirit and that the Spirit in you is the *same* Spirit that raised Jesus from the dead. No man can heal another man, but the Holy Spirit can work signs, wonders, miracles, and His gifts through any willing vessel. The key is to remain humbly transparent so God can flow through you, to His glory and praise.

4. See with the eyes of faith. Most Christians believe that God can and will raise them from the dead at the Second Coming. Resurrection faith is incredibly deep and grounded. But if God can raise a body from a pile of ashes, then God is certainly capable of healing and delivering people on this side of the grave. When you pray for healing, then you must trust God that He is good and He knows what He is doing.

5. Confess your sin before God and ask Him to wash you thoroughly in the blood of Jesus. David declared in Psalm 51 that it is against God and God alone that we sin. You should also confess your sins to another (who holds confidentiality sacred) and receive a clear, unconditional pronouncement of God's grace, mercy, and forgiveness. If there is any area of your life (heart, will, mind, flesh) that needs cleansing, then go into that place and seek God's forgiveness.

6. Proceed with expectancy. Too often people pray with an attitude of wishful thinking, but without expectancy. When you go to your physician, you have an expectancy that the physician will provide a diagnosis and remedy for the malady. You must have even a greater sense of expectancy with *Yahweh Rophka*, the "Lord Who Heals." He can provide the spiritual insight to provide the diagnosis and the divine remedy for healing. Have expectancy!

7. Do not give up. Luke 18:1 says: *"Then He* [Jesus] *spoke a parable to them, that men always ought to pray and not lose heart* [give up].*"* Pray without ceasing. Remember that once Daniel realized that the children of Israel had passed their prophetic deadline for deliverance, he began to pray. Twenty-one days later, the angel arrived to announce that his prayers had been answered. Daniel inquired as to why the angel took so long to arrive. The response was insightful, even for today's intercessors. The angel said it took twenty days to fight through the prince of Persia to come to Daniel. You, too, are warring, not against flesh and blood, but against powers and principalities. Pray and trust God to answer in His time.

8. Know your source of authority. When you engage in deliverance ministry, you must know that the power of the name of Jesus is greater than any demon. God created man with a free will, which he can exercise at any time. When Jesus would tell someone not to go away and tell what he had experienced, that person could choose to obey or not obey Jesus. They could choose because of their free will. Demons do not have that free will. When Jesus told a demon to go, they had to leave. They would often go kicking and screaming, but they had to obey. When you are casting out demons, you must know and move in the authority of the name of Jesus that the demons will flee.

18

Key Facts for Ministry

I truly believed that twenty-one days after my stroke, God would heal me. I attended a healing meeting expecting God to heal me completely there, and, indeed, I was healed. What I did not expect to receive was an impartation to move from that day forward in healing and deliverance. That particular outcome of the stroke was a total surprise. During the next few days, I pondered my healing experience as well as what it meant to receive a "mantle for healing and deliverance," the very bold words spoken by Pastor Hinn over me. While seeking God's will to walk out this new anointing, God clearly impressed on my heart that Rivers and I were to teach healing and deliverance around the world, to demonstrate the power of God at every opportunity, and to pray for others to receive the same gifting for healing and deliverance ministry. God told me that what we had been given, we should impart to others. With God on our side, nothing—even supernatural miracles—is impossible. However, as it clearly states in Hosea 4:6, *"My people are destroyed for lack of knowledge,"* there are several points for consideration for those who desire to move in the area of healing and deliverance. First and foremost, it is imperative that this ministry is understood.

MORE THAN HOPE—CREATE EXPECTATION

There is a big difference between being hopeful and being expectant. I am not hopeful that Jesus has washed all my sins away by His blood; I *expect* all my sins to be washed away by His blood. I have never seen my sins being washed away with my physical eyes, but I accept this cleansing of all my sin by faith. Someday I expect to stand before God in a robe washed clean in the blood of the Lamb. I do not hope to rise from the dead one day; I *expect* to rise from the dead. I do not understand how a pile of dust can live again for all eternity with the Living God, but I believe based on Scripture and my faith that this is going to most certainly happen. There is a very big difference in God's view between hope and expectation.

Likewise, we need to believe expectantly that God will heal and deliver people today as He has been doing throughout Old and New Testament times. If He said it, we must believe it. Consider these words from Romans 6 and Psalm 103:

> *For the wages of sin is death, but the gift of God is eternal life in Christ Jesus our Lord.* (Romans 6:23)

> *Who forgives all your iniquities, who heals all your diseases.* (Psalm 103:3)

God says He will forgive all our sins and heal all our diseases. God cannot lie; therefore, we must expect Him to honor His Word. I have held gatherings where there was no expectation for miracles and very little in the miraculous happened. But when expectations are raised to the highest faith level, then anything is possible.

Learn to Hear God

We know from Scripture that Jesus only did what He heard His Father tell Him to do. If you are going to imitate Jesus, then you will need to learn to hear His voice when He speaks to you.

When you have an illness, you go to your doctor. The first thing you do is explain your ailment and symptoms with an expectation that after you speak, the doctor will answer. If the physician does not respond to anything you have shared and remains silent, you would become unsettled. Why? Because you would expect your doctor to say something! Why should you have any less expectation for God to speak to you when you are speaking to Him? God *does* speak. Too often, the difficulty is in not being able to recognize His voice.

Listening gets interesting when we consider that there are several voices that actually speak to us. It is mandatory that we understand who is speaking, and what their true motives for speaking are.

One voice that speaks to us is our own voice. This voice can be healthy or unhealthy to listen to. The problem with your own voice is that you can be too rational or subjective, and this is the easiest voice to hear; it will say only what you think you want to hear. When you hear your own voice, you need to seek objective counsel from another healthy, spiritual person, in order to sort through its meaning.

Another voice that speaks to us is the voice of others. Like our own voice, voices of others can be positive or negative, depending on their motives. God can certainly speak into our lives through other people (Scripture bears this out), but you must be discerning to know if they are speaking for God or out of their flesh or their own sinfulness. If you have any doubts, again, seek the guidance of a different godly person to confirm the message.

A third voice that is always ready to speak into your life is the one that belongs to Satan. His motives are always evil, and he will never say anything that will edify or build up. Satan will twist the truth, lie, deceive, and distort God's Word, with the ultimate desire to have you spend eternity with him in hell. The devil's motive is to separate you from God, not only in the present life, but forever. His voice is never good; it is always evil.

A fourth voice, and the most important that speaks to us, belongs to God. His voice is always good and can always be trusted, as He only wants to bless and build up. God may use His voice to rebuke us for our own good, but His motives are always pure. He will most commonly speak to you through His Word—the Bible—but He also can speak to you through dreams, visions, an audible or inaudible voice, unctions, premonitions, or intuitions. The method through which God speaks may vary from person to person, but the key is to recognize His voice and listen. Once you have a clear word from God, then you must immediately act.

I was born in 1946, in the first batch of babies that became known as the baby boomers. I grew up in an average, all-American neighborhood with twenty-two houses on the block and dozens of kids. Every mother on the street treated us neighborhood kids as though we were their own. However, one mother's voice stood apart from all the others to me—my own mother's. No matter where I was on the block, I could always recognize her voice amidst the others. Why? Because I knew it. I was familiar with her voice.

So also, as you spend time listening daily to your heavenly Father's voice, you will become more and more familiar with His voice and begin to recognize it over and above every other voice. He can speak to you through others, your thoughts, your dreams, the Scriptures—it does not matter. But when you know His voice, you will recognize it. Jesus said in John 10:27, *"My sheep hear My voice, and I know them, and they follow Me."*

Four Words: Humility, Patience, Boldness, and Obedience

I have found that when God speaks to me, there are four areas of response in my life that I must exercise. These four response areas are foundational to the development of Christian character. These are the same characteristics we discussed earlier, but they bear repeating here.

First is humility, which is central. God speaks of humility in Micah 6:

He has shown you,
O man, what is good;
And what does the LORD require of you
But to do justly,
To love mercy,
And to walk humbly with your God? (Micah 6:8)

It is God's desire that we walk continually in humility: *"Humble yourselves in the sight of the Lord, and He will lift you up,"* says James 4:10. The Word also tells us that God blesses the humble and resists the proud (James 4:6). Pride was the original sin of Satan, which forced him out of Heaven; therefore, pride is an area where Satan can come into your life to encourage you to "puff up," or take glory for yourself. The only antidote to pride is humility. When someone thanks me for their healing, I always tell them to thank Jesus because He is the healer.

A second response to walk in is patience. James 1:4 says, *"But let patience have its perfect work, that you may be perfect and complete, lacking nothing."* We must learn to wait on God's timing. There have been times when I have cried out to God for immediate results, but nothing happened. As difficult as it is to wait, I have learned to trust God. Sometimes, I believe God is testing my patience. Sometimes, I believe that the lack of a response from God is more about my need to develop deeper patience. A great Scripture that addresses patience is Luke 18:1: *"Then He spoke a parable to them, that men always ought to pray and not lose heart."* When I do not see the results I am seeking, I remember the words of Jesus—I must pray and not lose heart! Our family motto is: God is never late nor early— God is always on time.

A third characteristic we must move in is boldness. The early Church was abundantly bold, even breathtakingly so, as recorded in Acts 4:31: *"And when they had prayed, the place where they were assembled together was shaken; and they were all filled with the Holy Spirit, and they spoke the word of God with boldness."* We serve a bold God who demonstrates bold results. He desires for us to follow His example.

Lastly, we must walk in complete obedience. God blesses obedience and full obedience only. What do I mean by *full*? I have three grown children. When they would ask me for the car keys, I obliged them if they had been obedient; if they had only been partially obedient, delayed in their obedience, or outright disobedient, do you think that they got the car keys? Absolutely not! I never blessed disobedient behavior by my children. However, if they had been obedient, I freely gave them the keys. Our heavenly Father is no different. He loves to bless obedient children. Therefore, walk in complete obedience, regardless of the task at hand.

> *For the weapons of our warfare are not carnal but mighty in God for pulling down strongholds, casting down arguments and every high thing that exalts itself against the knowledge of God, bringing every thought into captivity to the obedience of Christ, and being ready to punish all disobedience when your obedience is fulfilled.* (2 Corinthians 10: 4-6)

When you hear God's voice, remember these four traits: humility, patience, boldness, and obedience.

19

Knowledge to Understanding to Wisdom

Then you will understand the fear of the LORD,
And find the knowledge of God.
For the LORD gives wisdom;
From His mouth come knowledge and understanding;
He stores up sound wisdom for the upright;
He is a shield to those who walk uprightly. (Proverbs 2:5-7)

The distinction between knowledge, understanding, and wisdom is critical as we move in the healing and deliverance ministry. It may sound semantical, but we actually make this distinction in the natural world every day. Consider the theory of gravity, for example. We have *knowledge* of the theory of gravity through experience—when we drop something, it always falls to the ground. We *understand* that the theory of gravity applies to us as individuals, for if someone were to jump off a tall building, they would immediately fall to the ground (and be injured, if not fatally so). *Wisdom* is applying the theory of gravity to the situation: Do not jump off a tall building if you want to stay healthy!

In the healing and deliverance ministry, we need to have knowledge, or facts, concerning each situation. Understanding the overall impact of the ailment on the person's life emotionally, socially, relationally, spiritually, and mentally is also imperative. Wisdom is exercising the godly application to the situation in lieu of your understanding of the facts. The Scriptures teach that if anyone lacks wisdom, they should ask God specifically for it and it will be done. *"If any of you lacks wisdom, let him ask of God, who gives to all liberally and without reproach, and it will be given to him,"* says James 1:5.

An older, well-dressed woman came for healing to a Wednesday evening service in our church. As she began to describe her problem, Rivers whispered in my ear, "Phobias." I looked straight into the woman's eyes and said, "Do you have any phobias?" She immediately let out a gut-wrenching scream, fell to the ground, and began to sob and roll back and forth. I bent over and anointed her head with oil and commanded every unclean spirit to leave her in the name of Jesus. She lay on the floor for an hour weeping and sobbing. Eventually, she got up and told us that her entire life had been riddled with fear and she believed that she had just been set free.

After the deliverance, I collected the facts (knowledge) and thinking (understanding) about her ailment; Rivers, prior to it, was given a word of knowledge (wisdom) concerning the real issue. I could have prayed for her physical health all night and nothing might have happened, but when we touched the spiritual nerve and spoke against the "phobias," liberation occurred instantly. Wisdom is the key to unlock action in any given situation—especially in healing and deliverance—as reported in Ephesians 1:

That the God of our Lord Jesus Christ, the Father of glory, may give to you the spirit of wisdom and revelation in the knowledge of Him, the eyes of your understanding being enlightened; that you may know what is the hope of His calling, what are the riches of the glory of His inheritance in the saints. (Ephesians 1:17-18)

20

Understanding
Spiritual Warfare

We live with two realities: the natural and the spiritual. The natural reality is where we live and breathe and have our being, but it is the spiritual reality where we engage dark, spiritual enemies. Paul expresses this clearly in Ephesians 6:12:

> *For we do not wrestle against flesh and blood, but against principalities, against powers, against the rulers of the darkness of this age, against spiritual hosts of wickedness in the heavenly places.*

While standing on a boat looking into the tropical waters of the Caribbean Sea, you can see fifty feet to the bottom. The water is clear and sparkling, and the sunlight reflects brightly off the ocean floor. However, when you put on a mask and dive into the water, the whole scene dramatically changes. A world that cannot be seen from above the surface explodes with the vibrant colors of the fish and coral. This is like the two realms we live in. Through our natural eyes, we only see flesh and blood. With spiritual eyes, we see the spiritual world with its beauty and with its dark side.

Jesus defeated the devil, death, and hell at the Cross. Yet God has chosen to fight the enemy with His Church on

Earth, as Paul wrote in Ephesians 3:10: *"To the intent that now the manifold wisdom of God might be made known by the church to the principalities and powers in the heavenly places."* It is God's plan and will to humiliate the devil by using His Church to fight His battles. He encourages all believers to remember that the power of the Holy Spirit in us is greater than the enemy we oppose, as declared in 1 John 4:4: *"You are of God, little children, and have overcome them, because He who is in you is greater than he who is in the world."* Followers of Jesus must realize that even though we have a greater power in us, we still need to draw on God's grace and mercy and strength. *"Not by might nor by power, but by My Spirit,"* says Zechariah 4:6.

In 2006, a group of us were driving to a remote village in the mountains of western China. Two of my companions were a young couple, Pete and Francis. Another traveling companion was a U.S. businessman who loved the Lord and had introduced me to many ministry opportunities in China. The four of us, with a driver, made our way tediously along a rocky road that followed the Yellow River through a remote and treeless area of the Tibetan plateau. As we traveled higher into the mountains, Buddhism clearly dominated the landscape, as was reflected in the large number of Buddhist temples. We started out at eight thousand feet and climbed to twelve thousand feet. The sky was crystal clear, and the autumn air was brisk.

As we drove, I began to experience a severe pain in my lower back. No matter how I twisted or turned, I could not find a position that would give me relief. Since I do not have a back problem, this pain seemed totally unusual. I had the driver stop the car a couple of times so I could get out of the car and stretch, to no avail. Nothing seemed to give me relief. As we were nearing our final forty kilometers to the village, I had the driver stop the car one more time. I stepped out of the vehicle, followed by Pete, who emerged from the backseat with Francis. Without warning, Pete collapsed to the ground and appeared to have a major seizure or epileptic fit. I quickly knelt down to see if he was choking on his tongue, but he just writhed on the ground, blankly staring at us. After a few moments he stopped shaking and tried to stand up, but he could not get to his feet. Pete had never experienced anything like that before in his life, nor was he an epileptic. We waited a few minutes until Pete relaxed and calmed down. Eventually, he seemed normal—perplexed but normal. We prayed over him and got back in the car. As we drove toward the village, I realized that my back pain was gone.

When we arrived in the village, we met up with a young man who had been ministering in the region for seven years. He had only two converts to Jesus to show for his devoted efforts, and the second convert had only recently given his life to Jesus. The missionary spoke of his ministry, his hopes and dreams, and then began a tour of the village. When we shared the episode on the road with him, he suggested that it could have been a spiritual attack against us, for the region was very dark and heavy-laden with spiritual warfare. Of course, it made perfect sense to us. We had been under spiritual attack en route because the demonic realm did not want us to get into that village. When the light of Christ comes, three things will happen:

1. There will be an attempt to flee the light.

2. Some will come into the light for salvation.

3. Forces will come against the light to put it out.

I believe we encountered the latter as we approached the village. The demonic realm did not want us to bring the light into the area. Spiritual attacks such as ours will always come against the Church because we are God's vessel to fight the enemy. In the midst of every spiritual attack, the followers of Jesus must remember Paul's admonition in 2 Corinthians 15:

> *Death is swallowed up in victory. O Death, where is your sting? O Hades, where is your victory?*

> *The sting of death is sin, and the strength of sin is the law. But thanks be to God, who gives us the victory through our Lord Jesus Christ. Therefore, my beloved brethren, be steadfast, immovable, always abounding in the work of the Lord, knowing that your labor is not in vain in the Lord.* (1 Corinthians 15:54-58)

21

The Spiritual Roots
of Illness

The question the world loves to ask is, why are not all the people healed? The answer to this question is a mystery. While we can speculate, only God knows why He heals some and not others.

> *Who has directed the Spirit of the LORD, or as His counselor has taught Him? With whom did He take counsel, and who instructed Him, and taught Him in the path of justice? Who taught Him knowledge, and showed Him the way of understanding?* (Isaiah 40:13-14)

One truth we do know is that the root cause of death is sin. We also know that sickness is often a precursor to death. To go even further, I believe that accidents and injuries are the consequence of fallen humankind and sin. But we can still overcome. It is God's desire that we live and have life abundantly, as Jesus declares in John 20:31: *"... but these are written that you may believe that Jesus is the Christ, the Son of God, and that believing you may have life in His name."*

I believe that unresolved sin in a person's life can block the flow of healing. Again, we have a natural experience that can illustrate the spiritual. In the cardiovascular system, the blood needs unrestricted channels to carry oxygen and carbon dioxide throughout the body. If plaque develops in these channels, the flow of blood is restricted, which could lead to a heart attack. The medical solution is to clear the obstruction from the veins or arteries by inserting a stent or by replacing the vessel in bypass surgery. In the natural, unless a medical procedure is done, the person with obstructed blood vessels is at risk. Spiritual plaque, which can build up in our lives through unrepentant sin, must be eliminated. When we harbor sin in our lives, we literally block the flow of the blood of Jesus and ultimately, we prevent healing. Understanding the various spiritual roots of illness and injuries is essential if we are going to allow God to work through us in the healing and deliverance ministry.

Fear is one such debilitating emotion that is "plaque" producing. When angels appeared to people throughout history, the first words they spoke were, "Fear not!" Why? A holy presence invokes fear in unholy people. Joshua, Isaiah, the shepherds, Zacharias, Mary, and Peter, at first exposure to the holy, all felt fear. But God is love (1 John 4:16), and perfect love casts out fear (1 John 4:18). The Father pours out His love by the Holy Spirit into our hearts (Romans 5:5) to soak us in love and flush out fear.

What are the fears that build up plaque in us? Fear of abandonment, of rejection, of people, of failing, to start a very long list. The antidote to this sin blockage is God's perfect love.

Unforgiveness, which births bitterness, resentment, anger, hatred, and sometimes even murder, is also disease producing. And, of course, it does not please God. Jesus spoke about the need to forgive many times in His ministry. One clear example is in Matthew 6:14-15, in which He said, *"For if you forgive men their trespasses, your heavenly Father will also forgive you. But if you do not forgive men their trespasses, neither will your Father forgive your trespasses."*

Unforgiveness of self can lead to self-hatred, self-rejection, self-loathing, and even self-death. The only avenue of escape is forgiveness: of self and others.

Stress breeds the ungodly emotions of anxiety and worry. Jesus said in Matthew 6:25, *"Therefore I say to you, do not worry about your life."* The antidote to stress, including anxiety and worry, is supernatural peace, which can only come from God. When godly peace rests on a person, it breaks the strongholds of anxiety and worry, and a healthy life ensues. Peace, not anxiety, is a fruit of the Spirit. (See Galatians 5:22.)

Striving to please man (known as a man-pleasing spirit) versus God is a setup for rejection and ultimately the development of feeling personal unworthiness. As Jesus was nearing the end of His ministry, the Scriptures record several religious leaders who wanted to follow Jesus, but felt restricted by what people would think:

> *Nevertheless even among the rulers many believed in Him, but because of the Pharisees they did not confess Him, lest they should be put out of the synagogue; for they loved the praise of men more than the praise of God.* (John 12:42-43)

Today, no one is exempt from this temptation. Even pastors can be tormented by a man-pleasing spirit when they become more concerned about what people think of them than what God thinks.

Striving to find acceptance from a parent can also lead to a sense of unworthiness, failure, or rejection. A woman from one of our Wednesday night services illustrates this point. As a child, her father promised her that if she would go into the yard to pick clover and fill a brown paper shopping bag to the top, he would give her money. He instructed her to leave the bag on the front porch when she finished. He promised to inspect it in the morning. She faithfully labored to fill the bag and then dutifully placed it on the steps of the porch. The next morning, the father inspected the harvest of clover and found that the bag was not completely full. (During the night, the clover had withered and shrunk, causing the bag to be only partially full.) The beguiling father had his daughter inspect the catch with him, and declared that she had not completed her part of the contract. This broken woman told me she never received recognition from her father for a job well done. Sadly, she went through several marriages with men who also never affirmed her. Now in her sixties, she was still talking to her father, who had died twenty years earlier, trying to please him every night. Any striving to please man over God is a spiritual recipe for disappointment. But there is a cure. Matthew 6:33 says, *"But seek first the kingdom of God and His righteousness, and all these things shall be added to you."*

Lastly, curses on a person's life can cause problems in both the natural and supernatural realms. Curses such as substance abuse, divorce, and disease can flow from generation to generation unless they are broken. Curses also can be spoken against a person for the purpose of destruction. And people can even curse themselves by stating words like, "I wish I were dead," or even well-meaning words like "I wish I had become ill instead of my sister." The spoken word is powerful, and we must be careful with the choice of words we use.

I recently met a woman, Sarah, who told me that her sister, Cindy, had contracted multiple sclerosis (MS). Though both she and her sister were Christians, Sarah believed her sister to be more righteous and less deserving of such a horrible disease. She had even declared so in her prayers. Within a year, Sarah also contracted MS. After she told me her saga, I pointed out that God did not will for either of them to have MS. I invited Sarah to repent of the curse that she had spoken into her life. She did so, and I anointed Sarah and Cindy with oil and asked God to break the curse of MS on their lives. I believe in a merciful God, so while I have not heard from either of them in several months and do not know if they were healed, I have the godly expectation of a miracle.

The antidote to a curse is a blessing. "*Christ has redeemed us from the curse of the law, having become a curse for us (for it is written, 'Cursed is everyone who hangs on a tree'),*" says Galatians 3:13. Jesus is the one who hung on the Cross (the tree) and has broken every curse. If a curse is present in any form—past, present, or future—it can be broken by the power of God's blessing, for God's blessing is stronger than any curse.

Bearing the Scars
of Others

One of the most difficult emotional setbacks to the healing and deliverance ministry is seeing people not get healed. Every time I see people healed, I am elated. I pray that I never stop feeling the excitement and joy that comes through divine intervention into a person's broken life. The other side of the coin is equally emotional, but in a negative way. When a mother of twins, five-year-old daughters with muscular dystrophy, wheels them up to me for healing prayer, and she leaves with no obvious results and tears in her eyes, it breaks my heart. There is no way around the pain.

When people come to me and ask for an impartation for healing and deliverance, I always take time to explain to them the emotional downside to this ministry. I know God is good and always knows what He is doing. I also know I can trust him no matter what happens, but in the face of seeing a person not healed, I struggle … I shed tears … I ache…. And so will all who seek this mantle.

Sometimes God gives me a treat, and I get to see the results of His handiwork after the fact. I was once in the United Kingdom ministering in healing and deliverance. I had been at the same venue a year earlier and prayed for a number of people, including children. A man who was part of the event's worship band came up to Rivers and me to thank us for our healing prayer for his son. He told us that his son had been deaf in one ear and that Rivers and I had anointed him with oil and prayed for him to receive his hearing the previous year. The father related to us how after our prayer and during the course of the next few weeks, the boy's allergies had cleared up and his hearing was restored. We were delighted and encouraged to hear the report.

Rivers and I have learned that God is God, and we are only His vessels. If we see or hear about positive healings and deliverances, we are encouraged. If we are not privileged to see the fruit of God's labor, we are still encouraged! Why? The God we serve is mighty and big and great and awesome and powerful. With our God, all things are possible, including bearing the marks of suffering— even the suffering of others. I encourage you to put your hands to the plow and fix your eyes on Jesus, the author and finisher of your faith. He is the great I AM; the Alpha and Omega; the Beginning and the End; the Redeemer; the Healer; the One who came to make all things new!

How to Pray

How I pray for healing and deliverance in a person's life is determined by many variables, such as the location, the circumstances, and the number of individuals, to name only a few.

When I am in a position to anoint individuals with oil and lay hands on them, I will first inquire as to what is the healing prayer to be directed toward them. If the Lord gives me a word of knowledge concerning a spiritual issue, then I address it before I anoint them with oil. If I do not receive a word of knowledge, I then anoint them, lay my hands on them, and have them repeat a simple prayer after me. For example:

"Jesus, heal me of my _____. By your stripes I am healed. I receive my healing. I am thanking you in advance for the healing that I am receiving right now. I will give you all the glory and honor and praise. In Jesus' name. Amen."

We finish when I declare to them, "You are healed in the name of Jesus." I then ask them to see if they have any tangible results of a healing. Often God will immediately heal, and the person will sense or feel the evidence of this healing in their body.

At the end of a Sunday morning service, a couple came asking that I pray for their son. I inquired about their need, and they told me that he had injured his back in a high school wrestling match. He was experiencing back pain and could not bend over or sit for very long. I asked the son if he wanted me to pray for him and he said, "Yes." I had him pray the simple prayer for healing, and at the end of the prayer, I asked him to bend over and touch his toes; he did so several times. Each time he stood up, he said, "Cool!" I asked him if he could sit down. He did so several times and felt no pain. After hugs and tears, the family left full of the evidence of God's healing touch. Later in the week, the boy's mother reported that her son had not only returned to wrestling that week (at his coach's amazement), but he also had told everyone that it was God who had healed him.

I have seen this simple prayer work numerous times. But sometimes it takes a lengthier prayer process, especially in situations with large audiences. In a large, well-attended venue, it is impossible to anoint everyone with oil, so I have developed a more evangelical approach for healing and deliverance with the help of George Brandon, a Dallas businessman, who is spirit-filled and ministers in healing and deliverance. While not a definitive list, it is an attempt to touch all the necessary areas of a person's life as I walk them through the restoration process for healing and deliverance.

1. The beginning step is to settle the salvation issue by sharing the gospel and asking for people to accept Jesus Christ as Lord. At the same time, believers are encouraged to renew their faith and declare that Jesus is the Lord of their lives and the only source of redemption by His blood on the Cross.

2. Following the prayer for salvation, everyone is encouraged to humble themselves before Jesus as Lord and Savior, remembering that God resists the proud but gives mercy and compassion to the humble of heart.

3. From a posture of humility, people are invited to confess their sins before God. Everyone is encouraged to make an audit of their sins and present it to God. If they are uncertain of their sins, then they are exhorted to ask God to reveal every sin to them so that none may go unchecked.

4. The audience is exhorted to repent of all sins and to distance itself from any sins that they are aware of from the family's past; i.e., occult, false religions, unbelief, sinful behavior, etc.

5. The penitent is required to release all bitterness, grudges, and resentment and forgive all wrongs done to them by others. Forgiveness of self is also necessary.

6. By the authority of the name of Jesus, all evil spirits are then commanded to leave and go to the foot of Jesus for judgment: depression, fear, death, anxiety, lust, hatred, etc. Proclaim in the name of Jesus that all curses, or any assignments that the enemy has put on anyone's life, now be broken by the blood of Jesus.

7. A moment of silence is ushered in so that people can feel the liberating freedom that comes as people feel the load lifted from their shoulders by the power of Jesus' name.

8. Everyone is then strongly encouraged to begin to give God thanks, praise, honor, and glory for what He has done through the power of the Holy Spirit in the name of Jesus.

9. People are asked to place their hands on that part of the body where they need physical healing, emotional healing in their hearts, strongholds broken over their minds, or relationships restored. Then they are to ask Jesus to heal what needs to be healed by praying the simple healing prayer.

10. The hungry of heart are invited to ask Christ Jesus to place His hand on the person's head and baptize them with fire and the Holy Spirit and to immediately release every heavenly gift into their life.

11. The final directive is to make a covenant with God to amend each life today and for all to begin to walk in the newness of life that Jesus has promised for His followers.

These steps are effective and will always lead people into restoration. When they respond in a personal way and trust God at His word, restoration comes, and often with it comes healing and deliverance. Our primary goal must be to provide the opportunity for people to hear the gospel.

> *So shall My word be that goes forth from My mouth; it shall not return to Me void, but it shall accomplish what I please, and it shall prosper in the thing for which I sent it.* (Isaiah 55:11)

Part Three

The God of Salvation

For the wages of sin is death, but the gift of God is eternal life in Christ Jesus our Lord. (Romans 6:23)

If there is a firm expectation in every person's life, it is this—death. Sooner than later, your eyes will close, your breathing will cease, your heart will stop, and you will die. You can be healed over and over and over again, but eventually, you will die. Jesus raised Lazarus, the brother of Mary and Martha, from the grave, but because he was sinful, he still experienced a natural death. The wages of sin is death. No finite being will escape death.

The gift that God offers to all humanity is everlasting life—to be in His presence forever. The only miracle that truly matters is your spiritual healing, which comes through the blood of Jesus Christ. Jesus said in John 3:

> *For God so loved the world that He gave His only begotten Son, that whoever believes in Him should not perish but have everlasting life. For God did not send His Son into the world to condemn the world, but that the world through Him might be saved. He who believes in Him is not condemned; but he who does not believe is condemned already,*

because he has not believed in the name of the only begotten Son of God. (John 3:16-18)

When the seventy returned to give Jesus their report about how they even saw demons flee in His name, Jesus gave an enlightening insight:

> *Then the seventy returned with joy, saying, "Lord, even the demons are subject to us in Your name." And He said to them, "I saw Satan fall like lightning from heaven. Behold, I give you the authority to trample on serpents and scorpions, and over all the power of the enemy, and nothing shall by any means hurt you. Nevertheless do not rejoice in this, that the spirits are subject to you, but rather rejoice because your names are written in heaven."* (Luke 10:17-20)

I have seen many people healed from disease and infirmities. Rivers and I continue to witness demonic bondage broken in the lives of people around the world. We have seen the deaf hear, the blind see, the lame walk, and the impossible become a reality—many more first-hand accounts than space permits us to share. All of these signs, wonders, and miracles are exciting and astonishing and amazing. Great joy flows when the manifestations of God are present. Exuberance erupts from the crowds when authentic miracles are experienced. But all of these are for one purpose: to point to the Cross of Jesus. The real miracle is salvation.

In 2008, Rivers and I were in China. We had a wonderful visit to several cities, including Beijing. While in the capital city, we planned a tourist outing to the Forbidden City.

We walked through the large gates of the red- and gold-trimmed walls that towered above the walkway. I got in line to buy tickets while Rivers waited by the next set of gates into the main entrance of the ancient palace. When I returned, she introduced me to a young twenty-eight-year-old guide, Jon, who had offered his services to guide us through the Forbidden City. His English was mediocre but understandable, and we agreed on a price and began our five-hour tour of the palace, with Jon leading the charge.

The palace grounds spanned over one square mile. As we walked in and out of buildings, up and down stairs, Jon gave a very comprehensive history of the development of the various dynasties that ruled ancient China. He provided vivid descriptions of life in and around the palace. After completing our walking tour, we told him that we desired to see the Great Wall of China. He told us that in addition to the traditional tourist site, he would take us to another, less traveled section of the Great Wall that remained in good condition. He gave us a price for the tour of the Great Wall, and we consented and set a time for him to meet us with a driver at our hotel.

Early the next morning, Jon and a driver arrived punctually at our hotel. Our translator, Andrew, who traveled with us on our tour of China, joined us for this excursion. Andrew is a devout Christian. As we departed the hotel for the two-hour drive to the ancient section of the wall, I asked Andrew to witness to Jon and the driver of the van about Jesus. When the driver (who spoke no English) heard the name *Jesus*, his eyes darted to the rearview mirror. His interest was clearly evident in his body language. Jon told us that he had asked several people to explain Jesus to him, but they had either dismissed him or suggested that he read a book. I told Andrew that Rivers and I would pray for him as he shared the gospel with Jon and our driver in the Mandarin language.

Andrew shared the gospel message and his personal testimony for over an hour. As promised (and inspired, too), Rivers and I prayed intensely under our breath. I also videotaped the presentation with the handheld digital camera, as the moment was laden with God's purpose. At one point, the driver stopped Andrew to interject a comment. Andrew told us that the driver had attended a Christian meeting in the past, but he said that the people told him that he had to quit smoking to be a Christian. He felt he could not break his nicotine addiction and did not return to the meetings. Andrew continued to share the gospel with intensity and purpose. When he ended his presentation, both the driver and Jon responded in Mandarin. Andrew told us that they both were ready to accept Jesus as their Lord and Savior. We patted the men on the back and instructed Andrew to tell them that we would pray for them as he led them in the sinner's prayer. At the end of the commitment prayer, we praised and thanked God for the Holy Spirit's prompting and for these two new brothers in the faith.

We finally arrived at the old ruins of the Great Wall. Jon and the driver parked the van in the small village and guarded our backpacks while Andrew, Rivers, and I climbed down steep steps to a river. We crossed over on a ragged rope and wooden plank bridge and hiked up a steep dirt path to a section of the wall about two hundred feet above the village. After several hours of photo shoots and climbing a five-hundred-yard section of the wall, we hiked

Paul and Rivers at the Great Wall.

back to the village. Jon announced that our hard efforts would be rewarded: we would eat lunch in the village at a small restaurant.

The restaurant consisted of one table with the owner preparing our food. The meal tasted wonderful to our famished group of five. I enjoyed a tasty portion of what I thought to be roast beef, but Jon told me that it was donkey. After that, every time I chewed a piece of the meat, I thought of Mary riding into Bethlehem.

While we ate, Jon asked Andrew, "What prevents us from being baptized?" Andrew translated their request to me and I told them all we needed was water. I suggested returning to the hotel, where we could baptize them. But God inspired another idea in Jon. He told Andrew that he knew where I could baptize them in water, and we agreed to go with Jon's idea. He then bought two hand towels from

*Paul standing with Jon (right)
and the driver (below),
who were baptized
in the icey lake.*

the lady at the restaurant and we departed. The driver drove our group through the village to a large dam, parked the car, and then we all walked down a footpath to the dam. As we crossed over a walkway of old concrete to a dirt path on the other side, in front of us was a lake, formed by the dam. The lake was frozen. Sixty feet below on the riverside, the water trickled toward the old rope and wooden bridge we had used earlier in the day.

Jon and the driver walked down the dirt path to the water's edge. I stared at the frozen lake. *This is going to be interesting*, I thought. Jon and the driver picked up two large stones and scaled down an eight-foot embankment to the lake; they began to pound away at the ice, eventually breaking through to the water below. They cleared an opening about twelve inches wide and looked expectantly at me. It was time to do my part. I climbed down the embankment to the ice and baptized our Chinese brothers. With tears streaming down her face, Rivers captured the entire event on a small camera.

Andrew stood next to me translating as I baptized, and I could not help but think of the account in Acts 8:

> *Now an angel of the Lord spoke to Philip, saying, "Arise and go toward the south along the road which goes down from Jerusalem to Gaza." This is desert. So he arose and went. And behold, a man of Ethiopia, a eunuch of great authority under Candace the queen of the Ethiopians, who had charge of all her treasury, and had come to Jerusalem to worship, was returning. And sitting in his chariot, he was reading Isaiah the prophet. Then the Spirit said to Philip, "Go near and overtake this chariot."*

> *So Philip ran to him, and heard him reading the prophet Isaiah, and said, "Do you understand what you are reading?" And he said, "How can I, unless someone guides me?" And he asked Philip to come up and sit with him. The place in the Scripture which he read was this:*

>> *"He was led as a sheep to the slaughter;*
>> *And as a lamb before its shearer is silent,*
>> *So He opened not His mouth.*
>> *In His humiliation His justice was taken away,*
>> *And who will declare His generation?*
>> *For His life is taken from the earth."*

So the eunuch answered Philip and said, "I ask you, of whom does the prophet say this, of himself or of some other man?" Then Philip opened his mouth, and beginning at this Scripture, preached Jesus to him. Now as they went down the road, they came to some water. And the eunuch said, "See, here is water. What hinders me from being baptized?"

Then Philip said, "If you believe with all your heart, you may." And he answered and said, "I believe that Jesus Christ is the Son of God." So he commanded the chariot to stand still. And both Philip and the eunuch went down into the water, and he baptized him. Now when they came up out of the water, the Spirit of the Lord caught Philip away, so that the eunuch saw him no more; and he went on his way rejoicing. (Acts 8:26-39)

Andrew connected the two new believers with a Christian church in Beijing, and he has remained in contact with Jon as a mentor. I know the Holy Spirit immediately filled them with His presence and purpose for their lives. Just like the eunuch who returned to Ethiopia and birthed the first Christian church outside the Holy Land, so our hope is that God may use these two young men to birth a mighty work in China.

Rivers and I believe that the greatest miracle we witnessed in China rested with these two young men—they received the miracle of salvation. I know we will see them in Heaven, and I so look forward to that day. *"The wages of sin is death, but the gift of God is eternal life"* (Romans 6:23).